PLEASURES AND TREASURES

JEWELRY

Endpapers: Jeweller's workshop in the eighteenth century
from Diderot's *Encyclopédie*

CLAUDE FRÉGNAC

JEWELRY

From the Renaissance to Art Nouveau

Translated from the French by Donald Law de Lauriston

G. P. PUTNAM'S SONS
200 MADISON AVENUE NEW YORK

Acknowledgments

The following illustrations of objects from the Royal Collections are reproduced by gracious permission of Her Majesty the Queen, figures 1, 18, 37, 39, 44, 57, 69, 101, 121. The author and publishers wish to thank the following for permission to reproduce objects from their collections: La Comtesse de Rochambeau, figure 125; Lady Lucas of Crudwell, figure 54; Lt-Col Sir George Tapps-Gervis-Meyrick, Bart, M.C., figures 55-6; M. Lucien Baszanger, figure 79; M. Marc Garland, figures 103, 123, 134-5; Dr Helmut Gernsheim, figure 124; Lt-Col G. H. Hay, figure 38; M. Georges Sirot, figures 132-3.

The remaining illustrations are reproduced by permission of the following museums and institutions: Ajuda Palace, Lisbon, figures 85, 127-8; Bayerisches Nationalmuseum, Munich, figures 41, 70; Bibliothèque Nationale, Paris, figures 9, 10, 61; British Museum, figures 2-7, 14, 31, 33, 48, 51, 63, 75, 93; Fitzwilliam Museum, Cambridge, figures 13, 98; Galleria Nazionale, Rome, figure 32; Isabella Stewart Gardner Museum, Boston, figure 11; Kunsthistorisches Museum, Vienna, figures 15, 21, 28, 30, 45-6, 84; Louvre, figures 20, 27, 52, 59, 60, 74, 99, 100, 107; Metropolitan Museum of Art, Gift of J. Pierpont Morgan, 1917, figures 12, 16, 23, 29, The Michael Friedsam Collection, 1931, figure 110; Musée des Arts Décoratifs, Paris, figures 91-2, 105, 118, 126, 136-7; Musée Condé, Chantilly, figure 19; Musée de Versailles, figures 58, 78, 104, 129; National Gallery, London, figure 54; National Portrait Gallery, London, figure 72; Rijksmuseum, Amsterdam, figures 62, 64; Royal Collection at Rosenborg Castle, Copenhagen, figures 17, 43, 88, 95; Schatzkammer der Residenz, Munich (Bayerische Verwaltung der staatlichen Schlösser, Gärten und Seen), figures 40, 102, 130; Sidney Sussex College, Cambridge, figure 36; Sir John Soane's Museum, London, figure 47; Smithsonian Institution, Washington, figure 73; Staatliche Kunstsammlungen, Dresden (Grünes Gewölbe), figures 25-6, 80-3; Tower of London (Crown copyright, by permission of the Controller of H. M. Stationery Office), figures 71, 115, 120; Uffizi, figure 8; Victoria and Albert Museum, London (Crown copyright), figures 22, 24, 34, 42, 49, 53, 65, 67-8, 77, 90, 94, 96-7, 114, 116; Villa Reale, Poggio a Caiano, Florence, figure 50; Wallace Collection, London (Crown copyright), figures 35, 66; Wellington Museum, Apsley House, London, figure 77; Westminster Abbey, figures 67-8.

Other photographs were kindly provided by the following: Lord Twining, figures 76, 86-7, 89, 111-3, 122, 127-8; Messrs Sotheby and Co, figures 108-9, 117, 131, 138; Connaissance des Arts, figure 119; Alinari, figures 8, 32, 50; Archives photographiques, figures 52, 58, 74, 78, 104, 107; Giraudon, figures 20, 122, 129; MM. Josse-Lalance, figures 19, 27, 59, 60, 91-2, 99, 100, 125-6.

Printed in Germany by K.G.Lohse, Graphischer Grossbetrieb OHG, Frankfurt-am-Main
Library of Congress Catalog Card Number: 65-12434

Contents

CHAPTER ONE

Introduction

OVER the ages jewels have acquired an aura which fascinates human beings and probably always will. Their history is almost as ancient as the world itself; one could well imagine that Eve, being more conscious of her nakedness after the expulsion from paradise, felt constrained to adorn herself or to dream of adornment.

Jewels, and precious stones in particular, have long possessed a mysterious, even a mystic, significance which enhances their intrinsic beauty. Their durability is generally able to escape the ravages of time, and they possess a further attribute in that people can attach their own personal memories to them.

In man's preoccupation with jewels some have claimed to detect the birth of aesthetic feeling, for even the most primitive of peoples have used jewellery to adorn their ritual and magic-making ceremonies.

There is, however, a more practical side to jewellery. Their scarcity value and price have made jewels into symbols of rank, wealth and social standing for those that wear them; and because of their marketable value they represent an investment and an asset that is easily rendered liquid. This economic aspect, which is still valid, is one that has played no mean role in the history of jewellery.

1 *(opposite)* Portrait of Queen Elizabeth I by Isaac Oliver. The Queen is wearing the pearls given by Pope Clement VII to his niece Catherine de Médicis, and by her to her daughter-in-law Mary Stuart. Elizabeth acquired them after the death of the Queen of Scots

Antique jewels are rare nowadays, having mostly fallen victim to the whims of fashion in times when an object only a few decades old or less, simply became 'out of date'. It is only since the middle of the nineteenth century that jewels have become objects for the collector, destined to end their days in the glass cases of museums stripped of their primary function of adornment.

However attractive they may appear to us, the pieces preserved provide us with only an incomplete idea of the jeweller's art in the early periods. Often the only reason that the pieces have survived is that the stones are mediocre. The ostentatious pieces have disappeared because the more showy jewels they contained were sufficiently attractive for the piece to be broken up, reset and remounted to suit the tastes of a new age for jewels of great value. For this reason portraits assume a real significance for the student of antique jewellery, since they alone can present an idea of the historical jewels which are mentioned in ancient texts but are now lost, such as those of Henry VIII and Elizabeth I of England, and those belonging to the French Court during the eighteenth and nineteenth centuries.

The portraits tell a story which is more alive and vivid than the valuable but uninspiring inventories, for the portraits enable us to see for ourselves how the jewels were worn and applied in a functional relationship both to garments and hair-styles.

The pendants and necklaces of the Renaissance, when gold was combined with enamel, emeralds, rubies and sapphires in a rich and warm harmony, only come alive when seen against the brightly coloured, heavy brocades enriched with gold.

During the reigns of Louis XV and Louis XVI pale and lively colours were preferred, and this heralded a taste for precious stones of a pale hue, such as pink and pale yellow diamonds. During the period of the Directoire and the Empire cameos went admirably with the cut of the dresses then in fashion, which had been created under the in-

2-5 (above and opposite) Designs for jewels by Hans Holbein

spiration of antiquity. And towards the close of the nineteenth century 'dog-collars' became characteristic jewellery for dresses, whose lines were created by tight corseting.

It will be observed that many of the pieces dealt with in this book are of royal or princely origin, and this is because jewels were for a long time the perquisite of a small minority, which alone had the means to acquire them. The sumptuary laws tended to render this fact, from the thirteenth century onwards, into something approaching a legally constituted appanage. In France an edict was promulgated in 1283 to prohibit citizens from wearing precious stones, pearls, and certain jewels of gold or silver; in England Edward III made a statute 'de victu et vestitu' which laid down the costume and ornaments that the various classes of society might aspire to: craftsmen and yeomen had no right to any jewels of gold and silver, and only nobles or merchants possessed of a specific income were authorized to own precious stones. Laws of an even more severe nature were passed in Spain in 1380 and 1404, and again in 1600.

In France as late as 1720 the Regent completely forbade the wearing of pearls, diamonds and fine stones, and furthermore, ordered jewellers to liquidize their stocks abroad, but this edict was not rigorously enforced.

These early edicts reveal the mentality of a ruling class whose haughtiness knew no bounds, and it was really only in the closing decades of the eighteenth century, and particularly during the nineteenth century that the bourgeoisie, then becoming socially and financially more powerful, initiated the creation of jewellery corresponding to their tastes and their means.

From the end of the seventeenth century golden and silver ornaments formed part of the regional peasant costumes in France, Italy, Holland, for by then some country people were well off and could afford such ornaments. Nevertheless ornaments of this sort have not been included here because they belong rather to folk art and folk traditions than to

jewellery, in the strict sense of the word. We have also systematically excluded articles which were not adornment in the strictest sense: the handles of walking sticks or snuff-boxes, although these last were frequently made in gold and studded with jewels.

For similar reasons finger-rings have not been included either, with the exception of one which is particularly interesting for the historical memories it evokes [figure 57].

The goldsmiths who made jewels tended to associate themselves into groups known in France as *corporations* and in England as guilds. There was only a slight variation in their conditions. In London, as in Paris, the guilds included, as well as goldsmiths in the literal sense of the word, jewellers and dealers in precious stones; Diderot's *Encyclopédie* lists three categories of the profession:

> By *orfèvre* it is generally accepted that one refers to a craftsman who works in or sells no article save it be of gold or silver; by *orfèvre-bijoutier*, one who works or sells jewels of gold; by *orfèvre-joyaillier*, we understand one who works or sells diamonds, pearls or precious stones.

Prior to 1776 in Paris, however, merchants who sold precious stones had no right to mount them, for until that date neither they nor the gem-cutters became members of the goldsmiths' corporation. The *bijoutiers* were dealers in novelties which they sold (but did not make), and as well as jewels their wares included objects of adornment and novelty in cardboard, textiles, metal and wood. The number of goldsmiths was severely restricted as was qualification as a master-smith; standards of workmanship and regulations for the instruction of the apprentices were equally severe.

In Paris the goldsmiths were one of the six privileged bodies called upon to represent the industries of the capital at official ceremonies; the goldsmiths' corporation had its own hall, a chapel (rebuilt in 1556 by Philibert Delorme and decorated with statues executed by Germain Pilon), and had, furthermore, a home for the poor and aged masters of the craft. The May Brotherhood, which had its origin in the particular devotion of goldsmiths for the Virgin Mary, offered each year to Notre-Dame a painting executed by the best artists of the period and similar confraternities were to be found in all the important centres of Europe.

The French Revolution saw the end of the corporative system and its replacement, in the nineteenth century, by one of free enterprise complete with all its advantages and inconveniencies. England kept, and still maintains, the guild system. Goldsmith's Hall, rebuilt in 1835, still preserves the rich plate of silver-gilt that is brought out for great banquets, and does much to promote good design in jewellery and silver.

This respect for tradition did not, however, hinder the development of industrial techniques in workmanship in France and elsewhere. With cheaper and more economic production artistic quality often diminished; but this point has sometimes been exaggerated. It is true that a number of jewels of the mid-nineteenth century, made up mechanically for a middle-class clientele are, both in inspiration and workmanship, mediocre enough, but beautiful pieces ordered from the great master jewellers were still being made by hand with care and delicacy by craftsmen every bit as zealous for perfection as were their predecessors.

6 and 7 *(below and opposite)* Designs for a bracelet and for jewelled pendants by Holbein

11

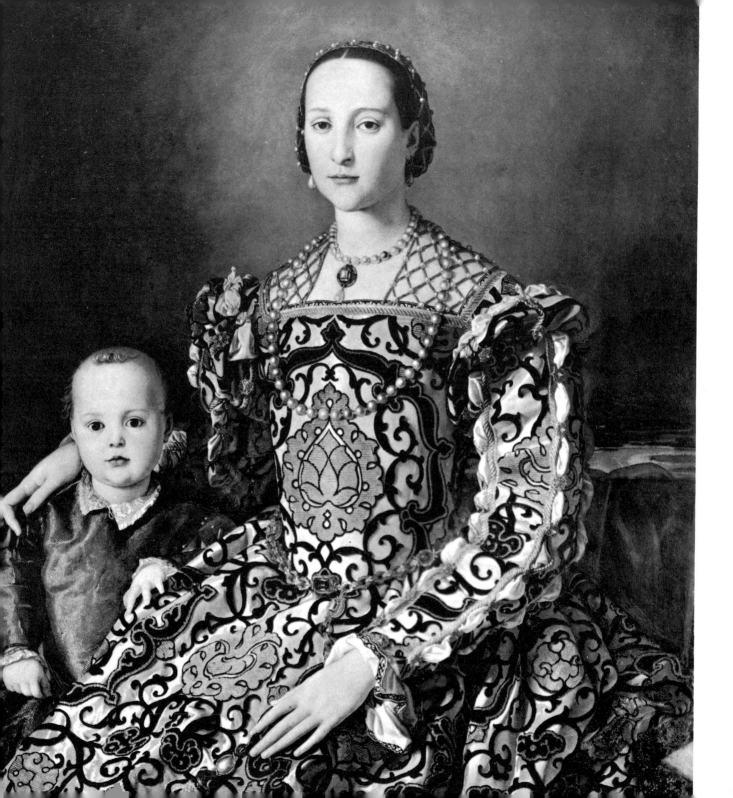

CHAPTER TWO

The Renaissance

THE wealth of inspiration which the Renaissance brought to Europe at the close of the fifteenth and beginning of the sixteenth century had a profound influence upon the jeweller's art. The new aesthetic ideals came from Italy, the true home of the love of the antique. This is faithfully reflected in the jewels of the period; and when one remembers that the workshops, the *botteghe*, of the goldsmiths were the schools where some of the great sculptors and painters of the Italian Renaissance received their training, it is easy to explain the beauty and quality of the jewels produced.

Ghiberti had begun his career as a goldsmith, before the end of the fourteenth century; after him came Botticelli, Pollaiuolo, Lucca della Robbia, Verrocchio, Ghirlandaio and Lorenzo di Credi, all trained as goldsmiths. In Germany, Dürer was the son of a goldsmith. Thus it is that in the portraits of the time jewels are portrayed with very great care, and with affection and understanding.

Fashions spread from Italy through Europe with much rapidity, and within a few years the stock subjects of decoration had completely changed; nymphs, satyrs and Olympian goddesses invaded courts and great princely mansions with their pagan seductiveness.

Engraved plaques occupy a position of marked importance in the midst of this exuberant activity. A painter such as

9 *(above)* Design for a jewelled pendant by Jacques Androuet du Cerceau

8 *(opposite)* Portrait of Eleanor of Toledo, wife of Cosimo de' Medici, with her son Don Garcia by Agnolo Bronzino. *c.* 1550

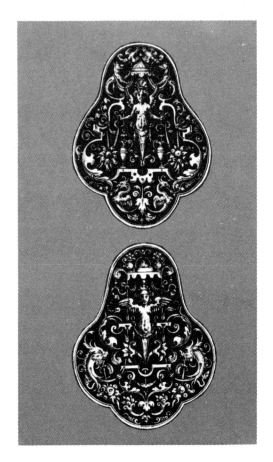

10 (above) Two designs for the enamelled reverses of pendants by Etienne Delaune. c. 1560

11 (above right) Portrait of a Lady in Black by Tintoretto (c. 1580), showing a necklace of wrought gold and pearls to which a pendant is attached

Holbein and an architect of the calibre of Jacques Androuet du Cerceau, did not disdain, to create designs for jewels [figures 2–7 and 9]; and other artists in ornament, some of them also goldsmiths, followed suit. The drawings of Virgil Solis (c. 1540) of Nuremburg, of Hans Mielich (c. 1570) of Munich, of Etienne Delaune (c. 1560) in France [figure 10], of Erasmus Hornick (1562) of Nuremburg bear witness to the existence of what might be called an international style, and indeed there are such strong similarities between jewels of this period that it is sometimes almost impossible to state their origin precisely. The problem becomes even more difficult when it is a question of identifying the goldsmith who made them. Contemporary documents do mention many gold-smiths, but for the most part these are nothing more than names to us. In this context it is of note that no single jewel can be definitely identified as the work of Benvenuto Cellini, considered now the most famous artist of his day in this particular sphere. We possess only the descriptions which the master has left in his writings and autobiography. Those show that Cellini attached much more importance to his *lavori di minuteria*, for altars or princely tables in gold, than he did to jewels in the strict sense of the word.

One point which stands out clearly in the pieces which have come down to us, is that precious stones played an accessory role in relation to the use of enamelled gold. Besides this the stones show but little variety in the cutting; coloured stones are frequently cut *en table*, flat, *en cabochon*, rounded, without facets and polished. Diamonds were usually cut as pyramids *en pointe*, flat cut, or rounded *dos d'âne* (donkey's back). Cut in this manner they could hardly show the fire for which they are famous.

Among the pieces of jewellery preserved from this time the most numerous are the *enseignes*, a type of medallion worn by men on the hat, and the pendants which were worn on the breast or as the central ornament of chains and neck-laces. Tintoretto's portrait of an unknown woman [figure 11] gives us some idea as to how they were worn.

The *enseigne* [figure 12] traditionally chased by Ghiberti for Cosimo de' Medici, would seem to be of later date; the interest in the piece primarily consists in the very sculptural nature of the medallion's centre representing St John in the Desert. This tendency is again evident in the *enseigne* [figure 15] which shows St John the Evangelist, in which the composition is on a grand scale considering the small dimensions of the piece. Another *enseigne* [figure 13] is nothing less than a minute gold bas-relief; the battle scene is handled with mettle and virtuosity.

In some other works enamel takes a larger place, partly

12 Hat ornament *(enseigne)* with figure of St John the Baptist in the Desert. Gold, enamel, pearls and diamonds. Italian, beginning of the sixteenth century

13 *Enseigne* with battle scene in fine gold *repoussé* work. Italian, beginning of the sixteenth century.

14 *(above) Enseigne:* Conversion of St Paul; said to have belonged to Don John of Austria. Gold, enamel and coloured stones. Probably Italian, early sixteenth century

15 *(opposite) Enseigne* with figure of St John the Evangelist. Enamelled gold. Italian, early sixteenth century

covering motifs and figures, bringing with it an attractive element of colour, but minimizing the fine quality of the chasing. This is the case with the *enseigne* which is said to have belonged to Don John of Austria [figure 14] which portrays the Conversion of St Paul; the profusion of figures, and the effects of perspective bear witness to a certain clumsiness of design.

The medallion showing the Entombment [figure 16] presents a better balanced and more solid composition which owes its origin to the Gothic tradition. To this same tradition belongs a rosary [figure 27] of which the agate beads open to show enamelled reliefs representing scenes from the Life of Christ. This appears to be of Italian workmanship; various other similar devotional jewels, which were in fashion in the second half of the fifteenth century, could be quoted as evidence.

If the religious subjects testify to the persistence, in Italy and elsewhere, of Christian sentiments during the Renaissance, the mythological designs are an expression of the pagan ideals of the new age. The *enseigne* [figure 19] showing Apollo and the Horses of the Sun owes its almost modern elegance to the unity of its background from which the young god and the rearing horses stand out proudly in half-relief. The border of enamel and vine leaves around a medallion representing Perseus [figure 17] is similar to that of St John the Evangelist, referred to above.

Simply by virtue of their shape the *enseignes* tend to monotony, but the pendants bear witness to a charming richness of invention. On the reverse of one [figure 18] Apollo and Daphne are to be seen amidst an abundance of intertwined foliage, among which sirens, boys and warriors prance and turn. The richly polychromatic combination of different enamels gives the piece gaiety and striking effect.

Ornamental designers and goldsmiths alike were provided by antiquity with a source of inspiration from which both profited greatly, but jewels dating from the Greek or Roman

16 *(right) Enseigne:* The Entombment. Gold, enamel and diamonds. Italian, early sixteenth century

17 *(below) Enseigne* with figure of Perseus. Gold enamel and lapis lazuli; head and limbs of the figure are ivory, and his shield is a cameo representing Venus and Cupid. Italian, *c.* 1550

eras were, in the sixteenth century, practically unknown, and could not serve as models, with the exception of some antique cameos, treasured through the Middle Ages, which were not only zealously collected but also imitated.

The fashion for cameo portraits spread rapidly. Moreover, the goldsmiths offered to princes and crowned heads likenesses which were not engraved, as the cameos had been; an *enseigne* showing Charles V [figure 21], dated 1520, wrought in enamel on gold, is a piece of virtuoso technique. More frequently the profile, like that found on medals, is in gold resting on a ground of hard stone; that of Charles V [figure 23] copied from a medal by Leoni, stands out against a plaque of bloodstone in a casing of lapis lazuli.

18

To our modern eyes these pieces seem collectors' objects — which, indeed, they have become — rather than jewels made to be worn; nevertheless they blended perfectly with the sumptuous dress in fashion at Italian courts during the sixteenth century.

Bronzino's portrait of Eleanor of Toledo, wife of Cosimo de' Medici [figure 8], reveals a taste which, while austere in its day, now seems elegant. On the sumptuous brocade of the dress the *parure* is composed almost exclusively of pearls, edging the transparent veil over the shoulders while two strings of very large pearls encircle the neck and fall down over the bodice. This refined but costly simplicity does not appear to have been widely cultivated.

The most varied and most highly imaginative forms are to be found among the pendants. One often sees pendants which represent ships [figure 24], and towards the close of the fifteenth century a taste developed for pendants in the shape of letters of the alphabet, generally the initials of their owner. The vogue reached its culmination in the sixteenth century. The list of the French crown jewels, drawn up during the time of Francis I, refers to one in the shape of a 'Latin A', doubtless belonging to Anne of Brittany. Henry VIII also possessed some pendants of this nature, on which his initials were joined to those of the particular wife of the moment. These pieces, probably because of their intensely personal character, have mostly disappeared, but two made for Anne of Saxony survive [figures 25 and 26]. Pendants forming the letters IHS in gothic characters are more common, although these are strictly speaking devotional jewels [figure 28].

The ambitions of Charles VIII, Louis XII and Francis I, in Italy, and the expeditions through which they sought to realise their plans, facilitated the entry of Italian taste and fashions into France; architects, landscape gardeners, and goldsmiths congregated on the banks of the Loire, bringing with them a reflection of the luxury and refinement of Italy.

18 Reverse of a pendant: Apollo and Daphne framed by entwined foliage, warriors, sirens and putti. Gold and enamel. Italian, mid sixteenth century

19

19 *(opposite) Enseigne:* Apollo
and the Horses of the Sun.
Enamelled gold and pearls.
Probably Italian, *c.* 1550

20 *(right)* Elizabeth of Austria,
wife of Charles IX. Clouet school,
c. 1570. She is wearing a *parure*
of enamelled gold enriched with
pearls and coloured stones

The luxury of the Valois court enabled them to make their living and, above all, to teach in France.

The Crown Jewels were formally created by Francis I by letters patent on 15 of June 1530, to form an inalienable treasure that each king had the duty of handing down to his successors either intact or augmented; up to the time of the Revolution the law was upheld with only a few rare

21 *Enseigne* with portrait of Charles V. Gold and enamel. Dated 1520

23 *(right)* Medallion of Charles V after Leoni. Gold and enamel on a base of bloodstone, in a framework of lapis lazuli. Italian, *c.* 1540

22 *Memento mori* jewel of enamelled gold; inscribed round the sides: 'Through the resurrection of Christe we be all sanctified.' English, *c.* 1600

24 (left) Boat-shaped pendant. Enamelled gold and pearls. Probably Venetian, second half of the sixteenth century

25 (right) Pendant in the form of a double AA, made for Anne of Saxony. Gold, enamel, diamonds and rubies. German, c. 1560

exceptions. Dangeau in the seventeenth century, referring to the 500,000 *livres* worth of stones offered to the Duchess of Burgundy, adds: 'These are diamonds which the king had bought but which he had not given to the Crown, because if they had been so given the king could neither have disposed of them nor borrowed them.'

The list drawn up under the order of Francis I shows a collection which is still in the embryonic stage, of which the most beautiful pieces came from the king's first wife, Claude de France, who had received them from her mother, Anne of Brittany. Several important stones are particularized, among them a large ruby called the *Côte de Bretagne*, the only piece that might possibly be traced today in the Louvre, although it was recut in the eighteenth century in the form of a dragon [figure 74].

In the institution of the crown jewels as a legal entity Francis I may have been motivated by a desire to conserve a fabulous heritage, but the economic factor cannot be lightly dismissed. During the reign of his successors, and specifically with reference to the expenses of the religious wars, a number of the stones served as a guarantee for foreign loans,

26 Pendant in the form of an A, belonging to Anne of Saxony. Gold, enamel and diamonds. French or German work after a French design. c. 1560

23

27 Rosary with agate beads, opening to reveal
scenes from the Life of Christ. Probably
Italian, early sixteenth century

24

28 Portrait of Jane Seymour, Henry VIII's
third wife, by Holbein. She is wearing a
parure of pearls, coloured stones and enamelled
gold and a pendant with the letters IHS

particularly from Italy. The correspondence of Catherine de Médicis enables us to follow the travels of some of the most beautiful treasures which were left as security, sometimes for long periods, with Florentine or Venetian bankers. These financial difficulties were hardly alleviated by the paroxysm of luxury indulged in by the last of the Valois. Upon the occasion of their marriage Charles IX's bride, Elizabeth of Austria, received no less than five complete *parures* composed of diamonds, emeralds, pearls and rubies. Clouet's portrait [figure 20] of the queen gives a very exact idea of their composition and the manner in which they were worn. She wears a *bordure* around her dressed hair, a *carcanet* (jewelled collar) encircles her neck, and there is a collar reposing on the shoulders; in front the collar is hooked up to the centre of the bust by a pendant.

Often the belt was enriched with jewels and ended in a long chain hanging down in front of the skirt. The chain would usually finish in a jewel, referred to in the old inventories either as the *patenôtre* or as *bague*, a word which we think of as meaning finger-ring but that in the sixteenth century meant any jewel.

Princely and royal dresses were at this time studded with pearls. The dress which Anne of Austria wore on her wedding day held ninety-two thousand. Catherine de Médicis went so far as to have the trimmings of her bed sewn over with pearls; these were not of great value however, being sold at three *sols* for a lot of ten thousand. They were rough and perhaps even false like those delivered to Elizabeth I of England. Henry III, on the other hand, presented his wife, Louise de Vaudemont, with pearls which contemporary chronicles report as fabulous, and which Henry IV bought back to offer to Gabrielle d'Estrées.

One of the few jewels which has been preserved in its original mounting, of which one may say with certainty that it belonged to Francis I, is a medallion showing Leda and the Swan [figure 30]. On the reverse it carries the royal

29 Pendant with figure of Prudence. Enamelled gold, pearl and coloured stones; head and hands of the figure are chalcedony. The reverse is enamelled with a design after an engraving by Etienne Delaune. Probably French, *c.* 1550

30 (*above*) *Enseigne*: Leda and the Swan.
Enamelled gold, diamonds and rubies;
the body of Leda is chalcedony. The reverse
has the cipher and salamander emblem of
Francis I. Probably French, *c.* 1540

31 (*opposite*) Book-cover, to be worn at the
waist. Moses and the Brazen Serpent.
Enamelled gold. English, *c.* 1550

28

ANNO · ÆTATIS ·   SVÆ · XLIX ·

cipher FF and the sign of a salamander. It was for a long time considered to be the work of Cellini, whom the king had brought over from Italy. He is known to have executed a medallion of the same subject, but the attribution is not so firmly held today.

The technique is characteristic; the head and the body of the woman are in chalcedony set on a base of enamelled gold. A pendant showing Prudence [figure 29] presents the same characteristics, in that head and hands are likewise in chalcedony and the reverse, which is enamelled, shows Diana in a *décor* of intertwined foliage: a reproduction of an engraving by Etienne Delaune. Even allowing for the fact that the drawings of Delaune may have just as easily been used abroad, these pieces seem to be French workmanship, and with some similar pieces suggest an origin from the same workshop.

Francis I had also brought from Italy Matteo del Nassarro, a carver of fine stone, who made several cameos showing the king's profile. A large oval sardonyx of Diane de Poitiers shows the degree of perfection which French craftsmen had attained in this field even although the author of the work remains unknown.

The court of Henry VIII was no less luxurious than that of Francis I, for the confiscation of the monasteries furnished him with enormous assets, lands and a large quantity of gold and precious stones. From the sanctuary of St Thomas à Becket alone came two chestfuls of treasure which some six or eight men could barely manage to carry.

In the majority of his portraits, for example that by Holbein [figure 32], the king is wearing a sumptuous collar of wrought gold, decorated with pearls and rubies — alternately oval and squared — which in their day were famous. His hat, his sleeves, and the front of his slashed doublet are ornamented with enormous rubies similarly set. The finest stones of the royal collections seem to have been kept for him, in spite of the fact that his successive wives received

32 *(opposite)* Portrait of Henry VIII by Holbein (1540). The King is wearing his famous ruby necklace, and his doublet and sleeves are also ornamented with rubies

33 *(below)* Pomander, which contained aromatics and was worn at the waist. Gold and pearls. English, sixteenth century

34 *Heneage Jewel* given by Queen Elizabeth I
to Sir Thomas Heneage. Enamelled gold,
diamonds and rubies. Miniature of the Queen
by Nicholas Hilliard (1580)

magnificent *parures*. These splendours have disappeared;
but some simpler jewels of his time, still preserved, reveal
considerable variety in design. Pomanders [figure 33]
which were worn at the waist and designed to hold aromatics
are an example of this; according to the inventory of crown
jewels drawn up in 1500 these musk-balls were equally
fashionable in France; no less than forty-five are listed.
Moreover some *parures* consisted almost entirely of hollowed
balls containing either perfume in paste form or ambergris;
these perfumed ornaments were much in vogue in France
but seem to have originated in the Middle Ages. They reveal
much of an epoch in which the most elementary rules of
hygiene were generally neglected.

Book covers had been made in gold or silver ever since
Byzantine times, but from the Renaissance onwards one sees
them hung at the waist; one of them [figure 31], its workmanship slightly worn away, shows on one side the Brazen
Serpent, and on the reverse the Judgement of Solomon.
Biblical subjects were greatly appreciated in England, although they were not restricted to that country. The *enseigne* [figure 35] of Judith and Holofernes appears to be
of British origin.

A portrait of Lady Frances Sidney, painted in the latter
half of the century, demonstrates how far one may pursue
research into costume; the figure holds a sable whose head is
worked with jewellery [figure 36]. Erasmus Hornick of
Nuremburg published in 1562 some patterns for jewels of
this type and some for fan handles, all richly decorated.

Towards the beginning of the sixteenth century the first
portable watches were made; according to the portraits of the
time they were then generally worn suspended from the
waist. At first they did not assume the very logical round
shape which came later, but tended to take on the shape of
the cross, miniature medallions, or the shape of reliquaries;
others, acting as it were as a *Memento Mori*, affected the
shape of a death's head.

35 *Enseigne:* Judith and Holofernes.
Enamelled gold. English, *c.* 1550

These death's-heads, crossbones, love knots, tears and other refinements, as Brantôme called them, were equally prized for mourning-jewels. There are some pieces, mostly of English origin, which were made in the shape of a coffin that opens to show a skeleton worked in enamelled gold. These generally date from the beginning of the seventeenth century [figure 22].

Elizabeth I of England appears in her numerous portraits rather like a distant and costly idol, bound about with the double aura of celibacy and power. These likenesses provide us with a fairly exact idea of her dresses and her jewellery, even if they are unable to restitute that exquisite charm of which her contemporaries spoke more convincingly than when they referred to her vaunted beauty. Here are to be found the *cotière*, necklace, pendant and, at first, the *carcanet* which gave way to the enormous flange-like collars in the final years of the sixteenth and the opening years of the subsequent century. From her father she had inherited splendid rubies and a large sapphire which she had preserved, as the portrait in the National Gallery shows, in the setting of the Tudor Rose. The fabric of the dress is strewn with pearls, but since an old invoice of 1569 mentions a delivery of five hundred and twenty pearls to the queen for one penny we know that not all the royal pearls were genuine. It seems to have become an established custom to present to the queen on each New Year's Day presents of jewellery, and the courtiers did not fail to comply with this costly obligation, which was probably a useful investment.

Nicholas Hilliard, famous today as a miniaturist, had been attached by Elizabeth to her court. He was an accomplished goldsmith, and grandson of goldsmiths, and it was part of his duty to help in executing the *parures* destined for the sovereign or given by her. The Heneage jewel [figure 34] is an example. This was bestowed upon Sir Thomas Heneage, Treasurer at War, as a thank-offering for his efforts to levy armies to resist the Armada. On a ground of translucent

36 (*opposite*) Portrait of Lady Frances Sidney holding a sable, its head worked in jewels. English school, second half of the sixteenth century

37 and 38 The two parts of the *cotière* given
by Mary, Queen of Scots to Mary Seton.
Gold, enamel, pearls and coloured stones.
English, *c.* 1560-70

blue enamel the front of the jewel displays the royal profile.
The reverse shows a storm-tossed ark accompanied by apt
inscriptions; when opened the jewel reveals a miniature of
the queen by Hilliard, dated 1580. The natural inclination
is to assume that the whole jewel is the workmanship of Hilliard, and to assume the same of the medallion bestowed
upon Sir Francis Drake [figures 55 and 56], a cameo of a
Negro's head with a miniature of the queen by Hilliard on
the reverse side.

Among the most sumptuous acquisitions of Elizabeth I
were the pearls of Mary, Queen of Scots, acquired cheaply

after the latter's death, which can be seen on Isaac Oliver's portrait of Elizabeth [figure 1].

These consisted of six strings of large pearls, and twenty-five pearls on their own but still larger, which had been given by Pope Clement VII to his niece Catherine de Médicis on the occasion of her marriage to the future Henry II in 1532. Catherine had given them to her daughter-in-law who had, in turn, taken them to Scotland after she became a widow. The jewels eventually passed to James I, and from him to his daughter Elizabeth, Queen of Bohemia, and then through her to her daughter Sophia, Electress of

39 *Lennox and Darnley Jewel*. Made to the order of Lady Margaret Douglas in memory of her husband the Earl of Lennox, who was killed in 1571.

Hannover, and through her they returned to England with George I; Sir Luke Fildes shows them in his portrait of Queen Alexandra. The *cotière* [figures 37 and 38] was given by Mary, Queen of Scots to Mary Seton; today it has been split into two parts, one half in the collection of the Queen, and the remaining half still with the descendants of the Seton family.

A miniature case of which the charming enamelled ornament shows the lilies of France and the roses of England has the inscription *Grace dedans le lis ha*; and it might have been given to Elizabeth of England by the Duke of Anjou, brother of Henry III who tried, in vain, to win the hand of the queen. The last six letters form the name Elisha. There was considerable fashion for these devices, which were often to be found with allegorical emblems.

Brantôme relates that when Francis I broke off his liaison with Mme de Châteaubriand he was weak enough to promise the Duchess of Etampes, his new mistress, the jewels of the former favourite who was particularly attached to them 'not merely for their value but also on account of the fine devices which were engraved or printed upon them' — these had been chosen and written by the Queen of Navarre. Mme de Châteaubriand then made a gesture which in its audacity was royal, she had the jewels melted down and sent the gold to the king as a gold ingot with this message:

> Take this to the king and tell him that it may be his pleasure to take back that which he gave me so freely, and which I return to him in gold. As for the mottoes, I have imprinted them so well in my mind and I hold them so dear that I could not permit anybody but myself to dispose of them.

We cannot form any true conception of the fine devices which Marguerite of Navarre invented, but the Lennox and Darnley jewel [figure 39] does enable us to perceive something of the very courtly subtlety which the fashion had reached in England — such subtlety as is to all intents and purposes lost to us today.

The jewel, which later belonged to Horace Walpole, was made to the orders of the Lady Margaret Douglas (niece of Henry VIII, and mother of Lord Darnley, the husband of Mary, Queen of Scots) as a memento of her husband the Earl of Lennox. The heart shape is that of the house of Douglas, and by virtue of its origin it should hold a miniature of the Earl of Lennox.

The clasped hands, the two hearts knotted together, these are clear symbols of married love such as inspired Lady Margaret, but there are obscure inscriptions, allegorical figures of Faith, Hope, Charity and Victory, a representation of the sun, moon, pelican, phoenix, a man standing between the sun and a laurel tree, and so forth. These had some subtle, secret meanings capable of recalling the moving episodes of a life of intrigue, and as such they remain unexplained.

This lively taste for symbolism, then current, was not limited to emblems and inscriptions but became connected with the stones themselves, and so continued what was already an age-old tradition. To precious stones had been attributed various magic or curative properties from the days of antiquity; Theophrastus' book affirms that emeralds are

40 Necklace made for Albert V of Bavaria, probably after a design by Hans Mielich. Used at ceremonies of the Order of St George. Gold, enamel, pearls, rubies and emeralds. *c.* 1565

beneficial to the eyes and similar assertions abound in the plentiful literature devoted to this subject during the close of the Middle Ages and the Renaissance. The works of Cardan, physician of Milan, of Camillo Leonardi (published in 1502 with a dedication to Cesare Borgia), of Marsiliano Ficino, of Jean de la Taille, all contain the most audacious theories, even though they are sometimes self-contradictory. The topaz, according to Jean de la Taille, when swallowed relieves melancholy; when placed in the mouth it relieves thirst; and sexual longing may be assuaged, we are assured, by placing a topaz on certain parts of the body. The carbuncle is endowed with the property of awaking a merry mood and other stones render those that carry them invisible, excite love, attract fortune or royal favours, and so forth.

One of the most valued properties of stones was their reputed ability to protect the owner from poison; this was one reason why they came to be mounted in jewellery. Jean de Troye records that the Constable of Saint-Pol, at the moment of mounting the scaffold, confided to the Franciscan friar who attended him a stone 'which warded off all poison and plague' to be given to his grandson.

Mary, Queen of Scots up till her death was carrying a black stone, the shape and the size of a pigeon's egg, having a cover of gold and believed to be an effective protection against poison.

Apart from precious stones in the strict meaning of the term, jewellery would sometimes have mounted in it, on account of their magical properties, snakes' tongues, sharks' teeth, fragments of a unicorn's horn (narwhal in reality), and so on. These same unorthodox objects, likewise mounted in gold, were employed on royal and princely tables to test and reveal the presence of poison, and as such are referred to as *languiers* or tasters.

The sun never set upon the domains of Charles V, Emperor of Germany, Archduke of Austria, King of Spain and all its colonies; these lands benefited from the wealth of the New

World, from the deliveries of gold and silver coming from the Indies which Europe greedily swallowed up. The great German towns such as Augsburg, and, towards the end of the century, Prague, basked in a pleasing reputation for goldsmith's work, as we may see from the list of jewels belonging to Claude, wife of Francis I, where there is mention of a golden *patenôtre* 'of German workmanship'. Nevertheless the style of these pieces belongs to the workshops of Florence and Venice; in the *enseigne* of St George and the Dragon [figure 51] only a few technical details permit us to detect its Germanic origin. The same might be said of the pendant showing Moses and the Brazen Serpent, with topazes, enamel and diamonds . This subject was extremely popular in Germany, England and Denmark. The Tau cross had attributed to it prophylactic properties which owed

41 Drawing by Hans Mielich, showing a jewel made for Albert V of Bavaria or his wife Anne of Austria

42 Pendant in form of a lizard. Enamelled gold and baroque pearls. Spain, c. 1580

43 Bird pendant. Enamelled gold, baroque pearls, diamonds, rubies and emeralds. Reverse enamelled in the style of Corvinianus Sauer. c. 1590

their foundation to a text in Ezekiel which stated that the elect of God should have the Tau upon their foreheads.

Some of these pendants hung from small chains and were designed to be fastened to the sleeve, as is shown in several portraits of Elizabeth I of England. It is thought that the medallion of the Annunciation [figure 59], a remarkably large piece (and undoubtedly from an Augsburg workshop) was originally designed to be worn in this manner.

The piety of the age frequently found expression in scenes from the Passion of Christ on a *parure*, like the splendid necklace [figure 60] of which the central pendant shows the Crucifixion surmounted by a crown surrounded by the collar of the Golden Fleece, which leads us to believe it was made to the order of Rudolph II. Of equal magnificence is the collar [figure 40] made for Albert V of Bavaria probably after a design by Hans Mielich. It is in fact very close to the artist's designs for jewels that were made for the Duke and his wife Anne of Austria [figure 41].

The imperial crown made in Prague by a Dutch goldsmith Jan Vermeyen, is perhaps the acme of central European goldsmith's work. It was made for Rudolph II in 1602, and belongs in style to the late Renaissance [figure 46].

The splendour of the piece is accentuated by the importance of the stones with which it is ornamented, which give an idea of the *parures* which have now disappeared, but were once ordered by the ostentatious sovereigns of the time. The crown is surmounted by a sapphire, and in the centre of the headband there is a large red stone which would seem rather to be a garnet than a ruby.

Clearly distinguishable characteristics can be attributed to a whole group of jewels dating from the second half of the sixteenth century; the sea monsters, dragons and sirens, executed with large baroque pearls mounted in enamelled gold, echo the drawings of Erasmus Hornick which appeared in 1562. The theme enjoyed marked success; they are not all of German workmanship but the most famous of them,

44 (left) Medallion: St George and the Dragon, traditionally belonging to Henry VIII. Gold and enamel. Spain, c. 1540

45 (right) Portrait of Elizabeth of Valois, wife of Philip II of Spain, by Alonzo Sanchez Coello. c. 1560

the Canning jewel [figure 65], is. The carved ruby on the body and the ruby on the pendant must have been added while the jewel was in India whence Lord Canning brought it back.

Pendants in the shape of birds also fall into this category; some were made in Germany, one of which [figure 43] has a reverse enamelled in the style of Corvinianus Sauer, a Bavarian goldsmith attached to the court of Christian IV of Denmark, and some in Spain dating from the first quarter of the seventeenth century [figure 66].

Spain was an important centre for goldsmiths in the sixteenth century, for it was enriched more than other countries by the discovery of the Americas. A medallion that can be attributed to a Spanish workshop, shows St George and the Dragon [figure 44]; it is, traditionally, said to have belonged to Henry VIII, and is one of a group of pieces with the same characteristics. The composition is in a heavy relief, enamelled with lively colour, ringed round with fluted gold. Although the austerity of costume was an extension of the independence of Spanish character, this did not hinder the princesses of the court from following certain French fashions so far as jewels were concerned; a portrait of Elizabeth of Valois, wife of Philip II, which was painted about 1560 by Alonzo Sanchez Coello [figure 45], shows the queen adorned with a *carcanet*, a *cotière*, head-dress and a belt similar to those worn by her sister-in-law Elizabeth, wife of Charles IX.

CHAPTER THREE

The Age of Louis XIV

RENAISSANCE goldsmiths were primarily chasers and enamellers; even in the most sumptuous jewels the stones arc enshrined and isolated by settings of gold which tended to take pride of position. About 1610–1620 there was a change in the approach to the jewel, the stone became increasingly appreciated for its own instrinsic beauty; considerable progress had occurred in the cutting, particularly where diamonds were concerned. From the last years of the sixteenth century comes the first mention in the inventories of cutting in facets, that is to say *en rose*; then in about 1640 we hear of cutting with sixteen surfaces. The goldsmith's art was yielding place to that of the jeweller; enamelled settings were reduced to the minimum and in the majority of cases went out of fashion for stones of real value, although enamelling was still used to decorate the reverse sides of jewels.

Berquen in his preface to *Les Merveilles des Indes Orientales et Occidentales* (1661) commented upon the change. The author was himself a goldsmith from Brussels who had worked in Madrid and subsequently became famous in Paris. He wrote:

> above all else before enamelling one should take care that the colours of the enamel could improve the stones and are able to match them. Diamonds need black, coloured stones require white and the variety of colours.

47 (*above*) Jewel in the form of a trophy, believed to have been lost by Charles I at the Battle of Naseby. German, *c.* 1615

46 (*opposite*) Crown of Emperor Rudolph II by Vermeyen. Gold, enamel, pearls, diamonds and coloured stones. The largest pear-shaped pearl in the centre is said to have been taken from the Terarequi Indians and brought to Charles V in 1515

At the same time the powerful inspiration of the Baroque gave rise to a taste for attractive and very luxurious jewels, a little massive in their magnificent amplitude.

A piece of jewellery of German origin [figure 47] presented by the king of Denmark to James I shows this new taste. This is believed to have been lost by Charles I on the field of battle at Naseby. It represents a cavalier armed with a sword and buckler in the midst of a trophy of arms. While the enamelled parts still have some importance, the way in which the stones are used to outline the various elements of the jewel is in itself characteristic of the new technique. A very fine devotional jewel, of Spanish origin, shows the same trend, [figure 49] and is noteworthy for the strongly architectural framework around the composition.

The royal crown of Denmark executed at a later date (1670) by Paul Kurtz for Christian V, although perfectly balanced, presents an impression of lightness: it embodies two splendid sapphires (the *Blue Mountain* is the better), and a number of rubies. The twisted scrollwork is of diamonds and stands out in relief against a base of matt gold, enamel being employed only for the orb which surmounts the branches [figure 88].

The art of enamelling was not entirely superseded by the new, increased importance of stones, and it attained a degree of perfection never equalled before. The enamelling of Jean Toutin of Châteaudun and of Jean Petitot, a Swiss who worked in both England and France, shows a remarkable finesse, especially in the portraits. The *champlevé* technique (enamelling done with vitreous powders in channels cut in a metal base) proved a success also. The extremely difficult technique of *émail en résille sur verre* only appears to have been employed by one or two craftsmen between 1619 and 1624; it consists of taking a medallion of glass (usually dark blue or green) and cutting the design in low *intaglio* to form the decoration, floral or other; the hollows are then filled with very thin gold foil, then above these

48 *The Lyte Jewel* presented by James I to Sir Thomas Lyte. Enamelled miniature of the King in a mounting of enamelled gold enriched with diamonds. Pearl pendant. English, *c.* 1620

49 *(left)* Spanish devotional jewel. Gold, diamonds and coloured stones. *c.* 1625

50 *(right)* Portrait of Claudia de' Medici by Justus Sustermans. *c.* 1625

enamel powder is inserted, using various colours, taking care that it vitrifies at a temperature lower than the glass plaque which constitutes the support.

Enamel survived as an ornamentation for the backs of jewels, and furthermore it achieved something of a triumph in two fields which, having first appeared in the sixteenth century, achieved a vogue in the seventeenth—watches and miniature cases [figure 48]. A French watch [figure 93] has a large *cabochon* sapphire forming its reverse side; the cover is composed of another sapphire encircled by smaller stones, and upon being lifted reveals an interior decorated with flowers, intertwined foliage and birds; it has a fragrant delicacy of composition.

Floral decoration became increasingly naturalistic, and began to supersede the stylized arabesques and figures of the Renaissance. The foundation of the botanical gardens in France by Henry IV became the source of new inspiration for the artists of the day. Among the numerous collections of engravings the *Livre des Fleurs* by François Le Febvre and the *Livre des fleurs propres pour orfèvres et graveurs* by Jean Vauquer (*c.* 1680) suggested innumerable designs based upon this theme. The pea-pod form was one of the first motifs to be used, and is seen on the setting and reverse of a cameo showing Louis XIII as a child.

Susterman's portrait of Claudia de' Medici (1625) [figure 50] shows a *parure* greatly influenced by the fashion for foliage, and is witness to the tendency towards naturalism which was affecting works of pure jewellery. The portrait has another point of interest for us, in that it shows in the costume itself the persistence of the tradition for lofty austerity, initiated by the Austrian and Spanish Habsburgs, still affecting the Italian court at this late date.

This same tradition continued in Madrid all through the seventeenth century; Velasquez painted Queen Maria Anna, the niece and wife of Philip IV, about 1650 [figure 52], enveloped in the vast hooped skirts still fashionable there, although outdated in France and England some twenty years earlier. Her jewels are few but massive and very large; they match her black dress and full, tight hair-style perfectly, so much so that one feels that the dress, *coiffure*, and jewels were all conceived together to convey an impression of majestic severity and soberly magnificent elegance.

Up to the end of the century in Spain the taste for heavy settings in which stones were set in scrolls and gold foliage held sway [figure 53]. This is confirmed by Madame d'Aulnoy in her *Relation du voyage d'Espagne* (1690); she speaks of the taste for 'earrings as long as the hand, and even longer' which then was found among Spanish women, and portraits of women, painted between in the years 1660 to 1670, depict this fashion.

In the gayer courts of France and England, however, fashion developed more rapidly. In England we see from Van Dyck's portraits from the court of Charles I that a more simple and more feminine elegance held sway. Lady Rich's parure consisted of magnificent, almost royal, but simple and massive clasps of large stones and pearls fastened to the front and to the sleeves of her dress [figure 54].

The king himself abandoned the sumptuous jewels of his predecessors. Van Dyck's portraits show him wearing only a single large, pear-shaped pearl in his ear, which according

51 *(opposite) Enseigne:* St George and the Dragon. Enamelled gold, diamonds, rubies and emeralds. German, *c.* 1550

52 Velasquez's portrait of
Maria Anna of Austria,
wife of Philip IV of
Spain. *c.* 1650

53 *(left)* Spanish breast-ornament *(crochet).* Gold and emeralds. *c.* 1700

54 *(below)* Portrait of Lady Rich (detail) by Van Dyck. *c.* 1637. *Parure* of pearls and coloured stones

to tradition he wore on the scaffold; Mary II gave it afterwards to the first Earl of Portland whose descendants still possess the jewel.

The ring of Henrietta Maria [figure 57] is another souvenir of the Stuarts; it is ornamented with a large diamond carved with her arms and cipher. The queen also owned the *Mirror of Great Britain* said to have belonged to Charles the Bold, which had been bought by Nicholas de Sancy. Having offered it unsuccessfully to Henry IV, de Sancy finally sold it to James I of England for the huge sum of 600,000 *écus.*

Henrietta Maria was soon obliged to pawn her jewels when she left her kingdom, and the *Sancy* was one of the first to go. In 1647 it was owned by the Duke of Epernon, and ten years later was finally sold to Mazarin. A letter addressed to her husband, then still in England, bears witness to the difficulties which the queen experienced: 'It is with the greatest of difficulty that we have raised any money here; the dealers are still nervous. News has come through from London that I have carried off the stones secretly against your will, and that if one loaned me money there

55 and 56 *The Drake Jewel* presented by Queen Elizabeth I to Sir Francis Drake in 1579. Front: cameo in mounting of enamelled gold, enriched with rubies and diamonds; pearl pendant. Reverse: miniature of the Queen by Nicholas Hilliard, dated 1575

57 Ring with square diamond, engraved with the arms and cipher of Queen Henrietta Maria, wife of Charles I. English, *c.* 1630

58 *(opposite)* Portrait of Queen Marie Thérèse, wife of Louis XIV. Seventeenth-century French school

would be no proper security. There was nothing for it but to show the authorization you signed.'

Mazarin, the all-powerful cardinal, was an avid collector of paintings, statues, *objets d'art*, and of jewels. He had matched together a remarkable set of diamonds, some formerly belonging to Queen Christina of Sweden; he acquired the set by purchasing them in successive deals, using funds raised by means which were often hardly honest. Upon his deathbed the cardinal asked his confessor to advise him how to make his will, and was told that he should render to the king all the things that belonged to him, but to distinguish between what the king had given him and what he had taken for himself; the dying man replied: 'in that case it is necessary to give everything up to the king.'

In fact the king refused to accept the whole of Mazarin's wealth, but among the part he did take was the *Mazarin* – the set of eighteen diamonds, and this became part of the crown jewels.

For the major part of his reign Louis XIV conducted what can be best described as prestige politics, and the effect of precious stones played a part dear to the heart of the man who liked to be compared to the sun. The crown jewels which he had received in trust from his ancestors now increased; the king acquired, in succession, the *Guise* diamond and the magnificent, blue diamond called the *Hope* diamond, which had been brought back form India by Tavernier. Later, having been stolen during the Revolution, it acquired a malevolent reputation as all of its successive owners, including Hope, died tragic deaths. The king also purchased a large sapphire of 132 carats now in the Musée d'Histoire Naturelle, and the *Hortensia* diamond of over 20 carats now in the Louvre. The king possessed no less than four complete *parures*, two of which were of diamonds, one of pearls and diamonds, and one, for daytime wear, composed of stones of many colours. The most important of these comprised one hundred and twenty-three buttons, three hundred button

59 *(left)* Pendant: The Annunciation.
Enamelled gold, pearls, diamonds and rubies.
Probably Augsburg, *c.* 1570

60 *(opposite)* Necklace made up of medallions
and pendant, with scenes from the Passion,
probably made for Emperor Rudolph II.
Enamelled gold, pearls, rubies and diamonds.
German, *c.* 1580

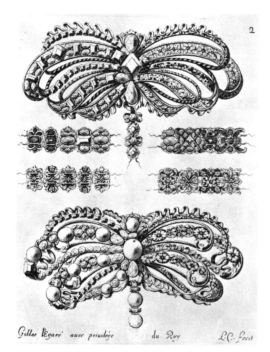

61 Designs for jewels by Gilles Légaré, showing the fronts of the pieces worked in jewels and the reverses enamelled. Paris, 1663

62 Stomacher in the style of Gilles Légaré. Enamelled gold, pearls and rubies. French or Dutch, c. 1690

holes, nineteen flower ornaments for the *justaucorps*, forty-eight buttons and ninety-six button holes for the *veste*, to which must be added, of course, the clasp of his hat, garters, shoe buckles, cross belt, sword, and the cross of the Holy Spirit.

With this in mind we can understand the description that Saint-Simon has left us: 'the King entered the gallery . . . his garments were ornamented with the most beautiful of the crown jewels; he was bent under the weight of them, he was wearing twelve million five hundred thousand *livres*.'

The Queen Marie Thérèse, although she does not appear to have been greatly interested in jewellery, and the princesses, notably the Crown Princess of Bavaria and the Duchesses of Burgundy and Berry, on grand occasions all wore stones from the crown jewels specially mounted for the occasion. The Duchess of Burgundy was described by Dangeau on the occasion of the marriage of the Duke of Orleans (1698): 'in a dress of silver tissue with golden flowers mixed with colours of flame and green. The *parure* of the head and the clothes consisted of diamonds, as did her necklace, comprising the most beautiful of the crown jewels.' The same princess, having played *Athalie* before the king, was obliged to take to her bed because the clothes she had worn on the previous evening had been too heavily laden with precious stones.

The king continued to make personal purchases of jewels for his family, especially for the weddings of the princesses of the blood. Madame de Montespan received some splendid gifts from her royal lover, among them a magnificent row of twenty-one pearls bought from the Maréchale d'Estrées and valued, so Saint-Simon says, at five hundred thousand *livres*. When Montespan fell from favour she returned the jewel to the king, who gave it to the Duchess of Burgundy, but in return aided the ex-favourite to acquire land at Oiron.

This display of splendour obviously provoked imitation among the courtiers who were continually changing their

63 Necklace in the style of Légaré (reverse). Gold plaques enamelled with black entwined foliage on a white base. French, c. 1670

parures to suit the fashion. As the *Mercure galant* affirms: 'people of quality change the settings of their jewels every two or three years'. Portraits show that masculine attire was as sumptuous as feminine. For men the main ornaments consisted of precious stones arranged in long, exaggerated button-holes with *Brandebourgs* or frogs. The *Mercure galant* describes the Duke of Orleans' coat at the festivities at Fontainebleau (1677) in this fashion.

It was not long before the frogs of diamonds spread to feminine attire, and the *Brandebourg* was seen to grace the bodice magnificently as complement to the brooches on the sleeves and skirt, to the earrings, and the single string of pearls round the neck, so big that it would seem that the painters may have obligingly exaggerated their size.

The engraved plates [figure 61], published in 1663 by

64 Reverse of stomacher [figure 62] in the style of Légaré, enamelled with a floral design

65 *(opposite) The Canning Jewel*. Enamelled gold, baroque pearls, diamonds and rubies. German, *c.* 1580

66 *(right)* Pendant in the form of an eagle. Enamelled gold and baroque pearl. Spanish, *c.* 1580

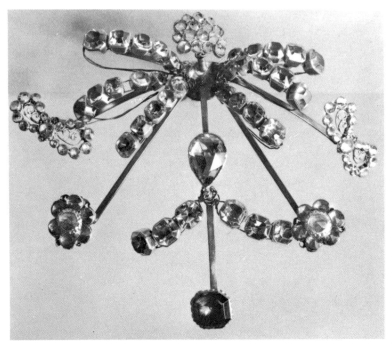

Gilles Légaré goldsmith to the king, who attained such renown that he was lodged in the Louvre, give a more precise idea of how the jewels were made up. If the backs still show an exquisitely refined enamel decoration the fronts are almost entirely made up of stones of various cuts and sizes set closely together.

Some pieces which have come down to us present clear similarities with these designs, but they are not so rich. One example of this type of work is a stomacher [figures 62 and 64] where pearls and rubies contrast with the enamelled arabesques on the reverse. Some necklaces show mountings of a similar style and are made up of plaques which have two narrow tubes on the reverse side through which the thread is passed to hold them together [figure 63].

Among the designs by Légaré one finds *girandole* earrings, sometimes having three or even five drops, and broo-

69 Pendant of gold and rock crystal. On the reverse an enamelled miniature of William of Orange in a frame of enamelled gold decorated with flower and leaf motifs. English or Dutch, *c.* 1690

ches in bow form, later to be known as *Sevignés*, but then called stomachers; the association of ribbons and bows with jewels was to reappear continually during the eighteenth and even the nineteenth centuries. Occasionally these bows are grouped to form necklaces *en lacs* a fashion that was to remain popular in England and Spain as well as France until the eighteenth century [figure 94].

The effulgence of Versailles spread all over Europe during the second half of the seventeenth century, except to Madrid and Vienna who stiffly held to their own dominating traditions.

Charles II and James II took to French fashions much more than their father had done. The revocation of the Edict of Nantes made France no longer safe for Protestants, and London benefited by the influx of Huguenot goldsmiths who fled there for refuge.

67 *(opposite left)* Wax funerary effigy of Frances Stuart, Duchess of Richmond. *Parure* of rock crystal, cut in imitation of diamonds. *c.* 1702

68 *(opposite right)* Hair ornament from the *parure* of the Duchess of Richmond [figure 67]

71 Regal circlet of Mary of Modena, wife of
James II. Setting made in 1685; the diamonds
were remounted for the coronations of
Mary II, Anne, George I, Queen Caroline,
Queen Charlotte and finally for Queen
Adelaide in 1831

The *parure* of the funerary effigy of Frances Stuart,
Duchess of Richmond [figures 67 and 68] is in fact of rock
crystal but it gives some idea of the magnificent jewels that
Charles II gave to his favourites. In a markedly similar style
we have the English or Dutch pendant mounted in rock
crystal, with a miniature of William of Orange on the
reverse side, worked in enamel in a setting of flowers and
intertwined foliage enamelled on a white base [figure 69].

The regal circlet of Mary of Modena [figure 71], the wife
of James II, was used for successive coronations by Mary II,
Queen Anne, Queen Charlotte the wife of George III, and
finally by Queen Adelaide (1831). On each occasion it was
remounted with stones especially borrowed for the ceremony, which were finally kept as they were in 1831, but
the mounting does not seem to have been significantly alter-
ed and shows the elegance of the seventeenth century in its
purity of workmanship.

70 *(opposite)* Heart-shaped socket for an
aigrette of herons' feathers with the initials
DM for Dorothea Maria, wife of Otto
Heinrich, Count Palatine of Neuburg.
Enamelled gold set with rubies. German,
c. 1600

CHAPTER FOUR

The Eighteenth Century

As from the beginning of the eighteenth century the history of jewels becomes primarily the history of precious stones, their beauty stemming from their selection, their cut, and the arrangement of the stones composing the jewel. They lose their objective character which is so evident in the sixteenth century, and a little less so in the seventeenth, and they become adornment in the modern sense, absolutely necessary to dress, closely subject to the changes in fashion; and furthermore there appears a distinction between jewels for day and evening wear. This idea took root in the final years of the seventeenth century in the gatherings of Louis XIV, the daytime jewels mostly being set with coloured stones while those for the evening were mostly diamonds and pearls which appeared at their best at the chandelier-lit balls and night revels.

The exploitation of the mines of Golconda, Ohio, opened in the seventeenth century, and then later of the Brazilian mines placed on the market more beautiful, bigger, more numerous and less expensive diamonds. The Venetian Peruzzi had invented brilliant cutting about 1700 and this development added to the progress already made with rose-cut stones. Henceforth the jeweller's art consisted in setting precious stones so as to gain the maximum effect from them.

72 *(opposite)* Portrait of Queen Charlotte, wife of George III. Studio of Allan Ramsay, c. 1762. The Queen is wearing a row of pearls, a necklace and a stomacher of diamonds, and has a jewelled crown at her side.

73 The great blue diamond, known as the *Hope*, which formed part of the Golden Fleece of Louis XV. It was recut in the nineteenth century

74 *Côte de Bretagne* ruby from Louis XV's Golden Fleece, recut by Guay in the form of a dragon

Jean Bourget in his book of designs (1712) gives very few designs for jewels because, he says: 'it is useless in my opinion because the fashions are continually changing, and furthermore the designs depend rather upon the quantity and the size of the stones with which one has to work.' In this field it is Paris which more than ever before led the fashion. With the accession to the throne of the Bourbons even the Spanish court, so long faithful to the details of a costume fixed by etiquette, began to adopt willy-nilly the French *toilette*.

French jewellers furnished a number of foreign capitals, and sometimes established themselves there, and in the Europe of the Enlightenment French fashions became still more influential.

The course of the century was to show comparatively little variation in fashion and called for very light mountings; the most popular motifs, subject to countless variations, being the bow and flowers. By the middle of the century such designs were influenced by rococo taste, although jewellers evolved a rather sober form of the style and, except in Italy, Spain and Portugal, generally speaking tended to keep to symmetrical patterns.

Major pieces of jewellery adopted a severely classical style round about 1760 as the rococo curves became less pronounced, and the researches of naturalists became more evidently reflected in the new way in which flowers and foliage were depicted. In 1788 Bapst made a jewelled bouquet of wild roses and branches of wild hawthorn.

The crown jewels of France constituted the most marvellous collection in the entire Western World, to which the acquisition of the *Regent* in 1717 brought a supreme consecration. The stone in question, weighing 136 carats, was then considered as the finest one known, having been discovered in Golconda and fraudulently smuggled out. Thomas Pitt had bought it in 1701; it had been cut in London and offered to Louis XIV who deemed it too expensive to buy. In his *Mémoires* Saint-Simon boasts that it was he who persuaded the Regent, Philippe of Orleans, to buy it:

> The Regent opposed the purchase on account of the state of the financial position; he feared being blamed for making such an expensive purchase when it was so difficult to provide for the most pressing necessities that many of the population were, of necessity, left in misery. I applauded this sentiment but added that one could not think of treating the greatest monarch in Europe as one might an ordinary commoner, and that he was obliged to consider the honour of the Crown and could ill afford to miss this unique chance to provide it with a priceless diamond which would excel all the rest in Europe.

Finally, after some bargaining, the matter was settled for two million *livres*, payable in several instalments, and Saint-Simon adds: 'The Duke of Orleans was agreeably surprised by the acclaim that the public gave to such a beautiful and unique acquisition'. The diamond came to be known as the

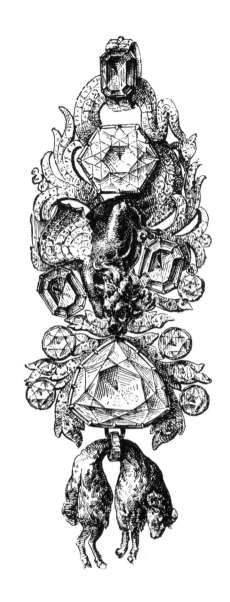

75 Reconstruction of Louis XV's Golden Fleece made by Pierre André Jacquemin in 1749 and broken up in 1792

76 Jewelled bouquet of Empress Elizabeth of Russia. Stems and leaves in emeralds, flowers in diamonds: one violet diamond, others white and some backed with coloured foil in pink and yellow. St Petersburg, mid-eighteenth century

Regent diamond, and Louis XV wore it for the first time on the 21st of March 1721, on the occasion of the reception of the Turkish ambassadors. It was set in a bow of pearls and diamonds fixed to the shoulder of his flame coloured coat, and in his hat he wore the *Sancy* diamond. These same two jewels are found again in the front of, and at the summit of the crown [figure 99] made by Rondé in 1722 for the coronation of the young king. The crown has been preserved and reset with imitation jewels of the time; it was then considered the acme of the jeweller's art, one of the first with open settings allowing the stones full transparency and so accentuating their luminosity. It bears witness to the short-lived taste for mixing coloured stones together, even to the degree of mixing fine stones with semi-precious stones, a characteristic of the eighteenth century.

The Golden Fleece made for Louis XV in 1749 is another luxurious example of this audacious mixing together of colours, and was to complete the parure of coloured stones which the king inherited from Louis XIV; today the piece is broken up, and is only known from the engraving [figure 75]. It consisted of the *Côte de Bretagne* ruby, recut for the occasion by Guay in the form of a dragon [figure 74], and the large blue diamond which has since been cut smaller and is today known as the *Hope* diamond [figure 73]; the two very large stones were surrounded by coloured diamonds and topazes. Much in the same spirit was the medallion of the Holy Ghost made by Jacquemin in 1757 for the king. Guay sawed a large ruby, the *Egg of Naples*, into several small pieces and gave them the shape of a dove surrounded by flames; this was set in diamonds, some of which were coloured by using tinted foil inserted in the setting behind the back of the stone. This method was not uncommon: the inventory of Madame de Pompadour also refers to 'diamonds tinted green' and 'yellow diamonds with assisted colour'.

The jewelled bouquet [figure 76], distinctly French, was made for the Tsarina Elisabeth before 1760; it is one of the most beautiful examples of its kind. Only the huge central diamond is naturally violet, the others are backed to show pink and yellow while the branches are set with emeralds.

For the large *parures* intended for evening wear the white diamond reigned supreme, in witness of which we have the cross of the Holy Ghost [figure 100] offered by Louis XV to his son-in-law Don Felipe, Duke of Parma or perhaps to his grandson Don Fernando, who received the order in 1762. A further example is the Golden Fleece made

77 Golden Fleece presented to the Duke of Wellington by the Countess Chinchon. Spanish, *c.* 1770

in Spain about 1770 [figure 77] and subsequently presented to the Duke of Wellington by the Countess Chinchon.

At the time of Louis XV's marriage the most beautiful diamonds in the crown jewels were remounted for Maria Leczinska; portraits of the young queen provide us with some idea of the sumptuosity of her parures [figure 78]. Generally she wore the *Sancy* and the *Regent* either in her hair or mounted and other diamonds in a necklace held tight to the throat by a ribbon of black velvet.

The adornment of the *grand habit* also comprised earrings, stomachers to cover the front of the body, shaped as reversed triangles, four-part girdles, shoulder knots, coat slits, hooks and eyes on the sleeves, bracelets in pairs, *trousse-côtés* and the *trousse-queue* picking out the sides and the train of the skirt held out by its panniers.

The jewels of the Dauphine Marie Josèphe of Saxony consisted for the most part of presents given her by her father the Elector of Saxony, by her father-in-law Louis XV, or by her husband (which was therefore her own personal property) and contained jewels similar to the Queen's but with less important stones. Many portraits of queens and princesses show how these *parures* were copied by most of the European courts.

The name of Marie Antoinette is forever associated with the affair of the 'Queen's necklace', a necklace which, in fact, she never possessed. It consisted of very large stones set in clusters with festoons drooping on the breast [figure 79]. The jewellers Baszanger and Böhmer received the original order to execute it for Mme du Barry, but it had not been finished when Louis XV died. It was therefore offered to Marie Antoinette, who refused it because Louis XVI considered it to be too expensive.

At this stage in the proceedings an intriguer enters the scene, the Comtesse de La Motte. She pretended to Cardinal de Rohan, who was then out of favour with the Queen (1784), that the Queen wished to be reconciled with him

78 *(opposite)* Portrait of Maria Leczinska by Van Loo. The Queen is wearing a diamond *parure*, and the pendant to the necklace contains the *Sancy* diamond

and would give him the responsibility of obtaining the jewel for her unknown to the king. The Cardinal handed over the necklace to an accomplice of the adventuress, believing the man to be a special envoy of Marie Antoinette. This man disappeared with the stones. Naturally the whole affair came out into the open, and Rohan, who was blameable of nothing more than incredible naïvety, was arrested, acquitted by parliament but exiled from the court.

The Comtesse de La Motte was flogged, branded with a red-hot iron, and flung into the *Salpêtrière* prison from which, however, she managed to escape. Though quite innocent the Queen came out of the scandal very badly, and Goethe referred to the episode as the opening chapter of the French Revolution.

There are many jewels which are said to have belonged to Marie Antoinette and the one which appears most genuinely to have been her property is the diamond necklace sent by the Queen to Brussels in 1791, and recovered by the Duchess of Angoulême in 1798. It subsequently belonged to the Count of Chambord, and Princess Massimo. It was sold in London in 1937, taken to India, and would seem to have been broken up recently.

Under the first kings of the Hanoverian dynasty the English court shone much less brilliantly than Versailles. Throughout the eighteenth century it was customary to hire the stones for coronation festivities, and as soon as the ceremony was over they went back to the shop from which they had made but a momentary departure. However they were hired in great number, if one is to believe the description, left by Horace Walpole, of the coronation of George II and Queen Caroline (1727). Her dress was so studded with jewels, so heavy and so stiff that she was quite unable to kneel down, and a whole system of pulleys was required to draw up the lower part of the skirt like the curtain at a theatre.

Queen Charlotte, wife of George III, possessed numerous

80 *(above)* Hat clasp of Augustus III of Saxony. Diamonds, with the green diamond of 40 carats at the bottom. Dresden, 1740

79 *(opposite)* Exact reconstruction of the famous *Queen's Necklace*, made in Paris by the great-grandfather of M. Lucien Baszanger, the Geneva jeweller

75

jewels, some of the most beautiful of which had been presented by the Nabob of Arcot. A portrait of her, painted about 1762, shows her wearing a necklace composed of very large diamonds, and a stomacher composed entirely of diamonds, as well as strings of pearls with bows at the waist and shoulders and pearl bracelets [figure 72]. These were to enjoy considerable popularity, and are to be seen in numerous portraits. Usually they are closed with clasps bearing diamond-encircled miniatures. Mme de Pompadour owned clasps of this type, engraved upon sardonyx by Guay with the profiles of Henry IV and Louis XV, mounted with emeralds and rose-diamonds. On one occasion the fragility of the thread of these pearls placed the favourite in an embarrassing situation, on the very day of her presentation at Versailles. Upon taking off her gloves to kiss the hem of the queen's dress, according to etiquette, she broke her bracelet, and her pearls rolled over the floor; the favourite, closely watched by the ladies of the court, knew that she must remain impassive, and retreated from the presence backwards, gracefully making the three customary curtsies as if nothing had happened.

Fascinated by the great lustre of Versailles, the large and small courts of Germany entered into a mutual rivalry in magnificence and refinement. In the deliciously rococo palaces built by king, landgrave and elector, festivity followed festivity and gave pretext for *parures*, which were hardly less magnificent than the French crown jewels. The vanity of the princes caused them to attach great significance to possessing some remarkable stone to be the star turn of their collection, and this would be mounted in a setting clearly dictated by the fashion in Paris.

Augustus III of Saxony, King of Poland, and father of the Dauphine Marie-Josèphe, had the celebrated green diamond [figure 80], weighing forty carats, set in 1740 in the clasp of a hat amidst a bouquet of diamonds suspended by elegantly waving ribbons.

81 (*opposite*) Epaulette of Augustus III of Saxony. Diamonds, including one of 48 4/8 carats. Dresden, *c.* 1740

82 (*left*) Rivière of diamonds belonging to the Electress of Saxony. Dresden, mid-eighteenth century

83 (*below*) Stomacher of the Electress of Saxony. Diamonds, with a central stone of 21 6/8 carats. Dresden, mid-eighteenth century

An *épaulette* [figure 81], a diamond necklace and a stomacher in the form of a bow [figures 82 and 83] made for the Electress and Queen, Augustus' wife, bear witness to similar elegance.

The Emperor Francis I, husband of Maria Theresa of Austria, inherited the pale yellow *Florentin* diamond (133 carats) from the Grand Dukes of Tuscany, and had it mounted in a magnificent hat-clasp. It is not known where this jewel is at the present time [figure 84], it was carried off by the Empress Zita at the time of the fall of the Austro-Hungarian empire.

84 *(left)* Hat clasp containing the pale yellow *Florentin* diamond of 133 carats. German, mid-eighteenth century

85 *(below)* Stomacher of emeralds and brilliants, with a central emerald of 47 carats. French or Portuguese, first half of the eighteenth century

The royal house of Bavaria possessed a Golden Fleece made in 1761 for the Elector Maximilian III Joseph, and in this the famous Wittelsbach blue diamond sparkled as the chief attraction [figure 102]. Previously the stone had belonged to the Habsburgs, and had been brought to the Elector Charles Albert (Emperor Charles V of Germany) by his wife, the Archduchess Maria Amalia. In the nineteenth century it was mounted in the royal crown for official occasions.

In Portugal both Kings John V and Joseph I were devotees of French goldsmiths' work; it was they who ordered the

luxurious tableware services from Thomas Germain and his son François-Thomas; they also had a taste for jewels. Some of the jewels made for the Court of Lisbon are beyond doubt of Parisian workmanship; but others [figure 103] reveal the competence with which Portuguese jewellers dealt with precious stones of worth which were entrusted to their care. Their style is, however, so close to that of Parisian artists that it is occasionally difficult to detect the origin of certain pieces of the treasures of the Braganzas. This is the case with the superb stomacher [figure 85] made up of emeralds and brilliants, the centrepiece being a stone of forty-seven carats.

86 Tiara made for Empress Elizabeth of Russia. Diamonds and rubies. St Petersburg, mid-eighteenth century

87 Clasp of the Imperial cloak, made for
Empress Elizabeth. Diamonds. St Petersburg,
mid-eighteenth century

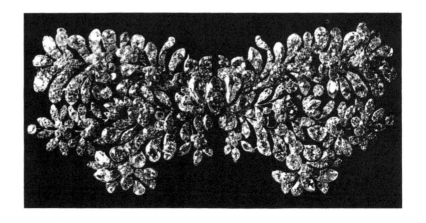

Such splendours are however overwhelmed by the all obliterating luxury of the court of St Petersburg. The Tsarina Elisabeth had ordered a clasp for the Imperial cloak [figure 87] about 1750, together with three other fine pieces in the French style [figure 86]. For her coronation (1762) Catherine II ordered an Imperial crown [figure 89] from the goldsmith Posier, of French origin. It was not ready in time but her successors wore it, down to Nicholas II. In 1772 the Empress acquired from Orloff, her lover, a magnificent diamond which was mounted in the Imperial sceptre and remained one of the greatest treasures of Russia.

Among the Russian treasures were complete ranges of little bouquets in diamonds intended to be sewn scattered on to dresses, together with borders entirely composed of large diamonds; complete *parures* comprising headwear, necklaces, *girandoles*, bracelets in pairs and much else of like nature, and sets of enormous stones — diamonds, coloured stones and pearls. These astonishingly rich pieces were obviously available only to immense royal or princely fortunes and most ladies of quality had to be content with *parures* that were rather more simple. But the beauty of French work [figure 123] and the delicacy of English pieces [figure 90], even with artificial stones, is remarkable.

In France Strass had given his name to a glass with a

88 Royal crown of Denmark. Gold, enamel, diamonds and rubies, with the *Blue Mountain* sapphire in the centre of the headband

89 Imperial crown made for the coronation of Catherine II by the French jeweller Posier, but not completed in time. Diamonds, pearls and a large ruby at the top of the arch. St Petersburg, 1762

90 Brooch in the form of a diamond bow. English, c. 1770

lead base which imitated diamonds with marked success, so much so that by 1767 the corporation of imitation jewellers had at least three hundred and fourteen members. Likewise, rock crystal was cut and polished either with a rose or brilliant cut; the necklace and ear clips illustrated [figures 91 and 92] are of Spanish origin but similar workmanship was to be found in England, France and Germany. Semi-precious stones were considerably appreciated for their colouring, among them agate, garnet, chrysolite and cornelian, and especially so in the *demi-parures* [figures 96 and 97] intended for daytime wearing rather than candlelight. Even women of high rank in society—the Duchess of Marlborough and Catherine of Russia to mention two – did not disdain to include them in their lists of jewels.

The attractive necklace of opals mounted in brilliants [figure 125]) which belonged to the Maréchale de Rochambeau, shows the care and attention given to mounting them; imitation opals were also made but usually in pinks and mauves which were unknown to mineralogy. Some of the most charming jewels made in non-precious metals are the

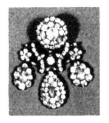 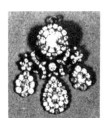

91 and 92 Necklace and ear clips with rock crystal in imitation of diamonds. Spanish, eighteenth century

parures of cut steel [figure 134], which enjoyed popularity in England and France in the late eighteenth and early nineteenth centuries.

Watches had adopted the familiar round shape in the second half of the seventeenth century, and in the eighteenth century they were manufactured in much greater quantity: they usually formed part of a *chatelaine*, to which were attached the watch-key, signet-ring, and sometimes various little articles for the *toilette*, flasks etc. The most luxurious are ornamented in diamonds, such as that made for Queen Caroline Mathilda of Denmark (1767) by the French jeweller Fistaine [figure 95]. Some are simply in chased gold or

93 *(right)* Watch of enamelled gold. French, *c.* 1620

94 *(opposite)* Necklace in gold, enamel, diamonds, pearl and sapphire. French, *c.* 1670

84

95 *Chatelaine* and watch of Queen Mathilda of Denmark (1767) by Jean François Fistaine, a French jeweller called to Copenhagen by Christian VII. Gold, silver and diamonds

pinchbeck, but most frequently they are the only jewels of the epoch to bear enamelled decoration and this adds to their interest [figure 98]. Many are decorated with mythological, *galante* or genre scenes, but their decoration changed as the century progressed, being strongly influenced by rococo about 1740 and closing with a pseudo antique style in cameo-painting with medallions imitating cameos. In England, especially, Wedgwood medallions were employed in mountings joined by chains that might be worn as a necklace as well as in bracelet form.

Jean-Jacques Rousseau brought about a fashion for sentimentality between 1770 and 1780, and this is reflected in numerous jewels dedicated to one beloved, to one 'close to the heart' or to the memory of a beloved friend or relative.

Dedications to friendship, doves, initials, funerary urns, weeping-willows were often worked in glass lockets in hair; the weeping-willow pattern was often effected in hair itself, and the fashion lasted well into the nineteenth century.

With the closing of the *Ancien Régime* jewels became in-

96 and 97 *(opposite and above) Demi-parure:* brooch and ear-pendants of chrysolites. Spanish, *c.* 1760

creasingly reserved to the feminine sex, even though the king at court continued to wear his diamonds on great occasions. The fashion for austerity spread from England. Coats covered in embroidery and spangles in light colours and shot silk gave way to the frock coat in sober hues of beige, brown, green and puce.

Shoe buckles comprised an essential part of masculine attire and there are a great many varieties from the simple, silver buckle dear to country priests, to the more luxurious in gold or even set with jewels.

Throughout Europe the young men of fashion submitted to the more severe styles prevailing, and henceforth the only jewels permitted were finger-rings, cravat-pins and the watch chain with the trinkets that belonged to it.

The bourgeoisie under Louis-Philippe and the Second Empire were to take to this fashion, so discreet and reassuring, with some enthusiasm, although at the same time stripping it of the subtle refinements which Brummell, Rastignac and Rubempré and the like had brought to it.

98 *Chatelaine* and watch made about 1705 for Queen Anne by Thuilst. Enamelled gold, mother-of-pearl and garnets

99 (*left*) Crown made for the coronation of
Louis XV in 1722 by Claude Rondé.
The stones, which are false, were remounted
after the ceremony. In the centre above the
headband is a copy of the *Regent* diamond
and at the top a copy of the *Sancy*

100 (*above*) Cross of the Holy Ghost presented
by Louis XV to his son-in-law Don Philip,
Duke of Parma, or to his grandson Don
Ferdinand. Diamonds, with the dove's beak
worked in rubies. Probably by Jacquemin,
crown jeweller 1757-73

CHAPTER FIVE

From the French Revolution to Art Nouveau

THE French Revolution marked the beginning of an unfavourable period for *parures*. Willy-nilly Europe found itself engaged in war. True the new ideology gave rise in France to jewels suitable for the events, decorated with Phrygian caps, pikes, fasces, and symbols of Liberty, but their quality is so mediocre that they never seem to have been intended to last for long. In so far as the crown jewels were concerned the results were tragic. In 1791 the king had deposited them in their entirety in the royal furniture repository (now the Ministry for the Marine) where they had been placed under lock and key, but whence they were stolen some time between the 11th and 17th of September, 1792. The robbers appear to have entered by the window so that the seals on the doors were unbroken. They therefore had six days clear to get away, and the loss was not discovered until it was too late.

Without any real foundation many rumours circulated about the robbery, among them one that the Girondins had, with the aid of the jewels, bought the support of the Duke of Brunswick, leader of the enemy forces, and so gained the battle of Valmy.

Following many denunciations, enquiries and much research the majority of the stones were recovered; the *Regent*,

101 *(opposite)* Queen Victoria by Winterhalter. The Queen is wearing the regal circlet of George IV, ear-pendants, necklace, *bordure* and stomacher in diamonds, and pearl bracelets. At her side is the crown of state

91

102 *(left)* Golden Fleece made for Maximilian III Joseph of Bavaria. In the centre is the Wittelsbach blue diamond surrounded by white diamonds. In the middle of the pendant supporting the Fleece is a pink diamond. Munich, 1761

103 *(opposite)* Stomacher in diamonds and emeralds. Portuguese, early eighteenth century

104 Portrait of Queen Marie-Caroline of Naples by Mme Vigée-Lebrun, c. 1806. The Queen is wearing a cameo parure with pearls

105 (opposite) Parure in gold, cornelian and pearls, made up of a tiara, paired bracelets, necklace, ear-rings, hairpin, paired rings and a small pin. French, early nineteenth century

it is said, had been concealed in a wooden beam. The great blue diamond of Louis XIV (the *Hope*) was already on its way abroad. The Republic, which never stood upon ceremony when its interests were at stake, sent five of the malefactors to the scaffold for the deed.

The treasury was, however, enriched by stones confiscated from the *émigrés* and also by those of the King of Sardinia seized in Holland as enemy property; they had been sent there as guarantee for a loan.

But the wars gave rise to financial difficulties and the French government was obliged to use the largest pieces as securities for loans: the *Regent* was placed with the banker Treskow in Berlin, the *Sancy* at Madrid with the Marquis d'Iranda, while both men furnished the Republic with much needed horses. The *Sancy* was never recovered, passing via Godoy, Prince de la Paix and lover of Maria Luisa of Spain, to Prince Demidoff and finally via India to the Astor family who still possess it.

By way of compensation the Directoire brought a relief from the recent terror; a feast of pleasure took hold of those who had escaped from the guillotine; at the Paphos and the Tivoli pleasure gardens the eccentric fashions of the *merveilleuses du Directoire* created a sensation at the dances, wearing thin muslin tunics over their half-naked bodies with a red ribbon *à la victime* knotted round their necks. There was a taste for very long earrings known as 'fishwives', a name which gives an idea of the feeling current at these festivities. Jewels were, generally, quite simple: few stones but long golden chains joined by medallions in the antique style adorned with enamel or cameos, called *sautoirs*. It is remarkable that the identical type of *sautoir* was adopted with equal enthusiasm by the flappers after the first world war during the twenties.

Some women, however, wives of eminent persons in the new régime, did possess valuable *parures*, as the following letter testifies, it is from the future Empress Josephine:

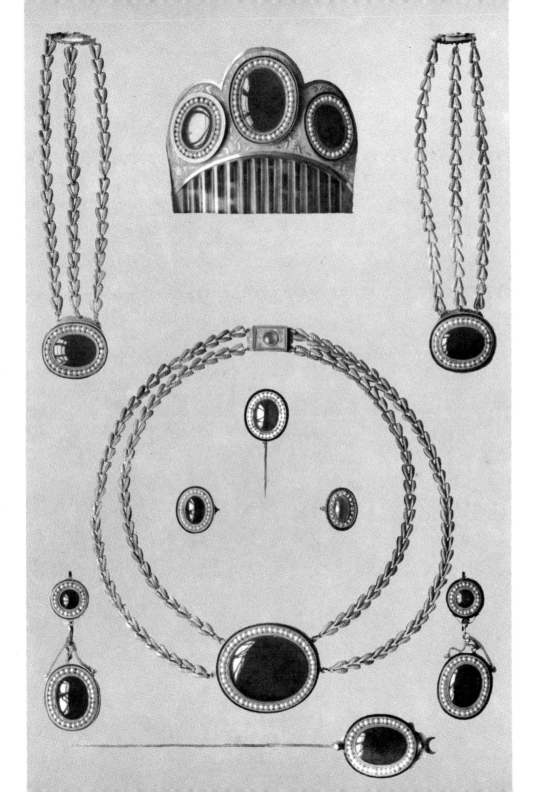

106 Stomacher supposed to have belonged to Queen Maria Anna
Victoria of Portugal, wife of Joseph I. Diamonds and rubies. Spanish or
Portuguese, mid-eighteenth century

Citizen! Oblige me by bringing tomorrow morning my diamond necklace for which Bonaparte believes he is pledged; in order to demonstrate the contrary to him, I want to have it at home. I wish you a good evening. – Lapagerie-Bonaparte.

The letter throws some curious sidelight on domestic arrangements in the Bonaparte household.

The Roman carnivals gave way to rigid fasts with the proclamation of the Empire under the new Caesar, and after his coronation Napoleon established a stiff court etiquette, similar to that in force under the *Ancien Régime*. Maréchales, Duchesses and Princesses aware of their new honours were generally very conscious of the need to uphold their rank with all possible dignity. Stiff satins and luxurious embroideries replaced the indiscreet muslins of the Directoire, and once again diamonds enhanced the court balls. Even when only first consul Napoleon had had Nitot mount the *Regent* on the hilt of a ceremonial sword. Part of the crown jewels had been placed at the disposition of *la citoyenne* Bonaparte.

After the coronation imperial orders multiplied, at first for Josephine, who in 1805 received a complete diamond *parure* valued at 347,800 francs; and after 1810 even more so for Marie-Louise who had six complete *parures* in pearls, diamonds, sapphires, rubies, emeralds and turquoises.

Portraits demonstrate quite clearly how full these *parures* were [figure 129]: each comprised a tiara set quite low on the forehead, a comb planted on the top of the head, ear pendants and necklace, not to mention belt and paired. bracelets. There were also crowns for the sets with diamonds and pearls.

The imperial magnificence was not exercised without a strict awareness of economy. On 8 January 1810 the Emperor wrote to Count Daru: 'I have no need of these *parures* immediately nor should several hundreds of thousands of francs be sacrificed for them. On the contrary it is

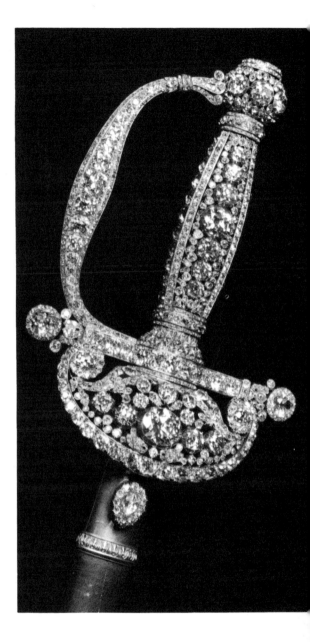

107 Diamond sword designed by Evrard Bapst and made by Charles Bapst for the coronation of Charles X in 1824

108 Tiara of the Duchess of Angoulême by Evrard Bapst (1816). Diamonds and rubies

my wish that they should be acquired without undue haste at the lowest possible price.'

These purchases, intended to rebuild and add to the collection of the crown jewels, were additional to the personal presents which the Emperor gave to the Empress and to members of his family, and to the daughters of his senior officers, etc.

Apart from ceremonial pieces such jewellery as was used for day wear was clearly simpler, like the fine *parure* of cornelians and pearls illustrated [figure 105].

The taste for the Antique brought back with it the fashion of cameos, Marie-Louise had an entire *parure* of this type, and one for which some of the finest sardonyxes were removed from the Cabinet des Médailles at the Bibliothèque Nationale.

The importance attached to cameos is emphasized by the *parure* worn by Queen Marie-Caroline of Naples [figure

104], for in the portrait by Mme Vigée Le Brun we see that they are encircled by enormous pearls. The *Journal des Dames* (1805) affirms:

A fashionable lady wears cameos at her girdle, cameos in her necklace, cameos on each of her bracelets, a cameo on her tiara. Antique stones are more fashionable than ever, but in default of them one may employ engraved shells.

Gold jewels, particulary the braided chains called *jaserons* enjoyed some popularity around 1804. The *Journal de La Mésangère* announced in 1805 the success of matted gold with rough filigree work *(canetille)*, this was especially recommended to the teenagers about fifteen years old who might wear a *grande parure* and tiara made of *canetille* gold and silver as being cheaper than one of brilliants, 'the overall effect is divine especially upon dark hair'.

The Ingres portraits of Mme Rivière and Mme de Senonnes, provide us with a fairly accurate idea of these rather unassuming jewels which were purely decorative, the equivalent, more or less, of present-day costume-jewellery. Berlin cast-iron jewels with medallions, chased openwork and a taste for neo-classical subjetcts fall within the same category; the medallions were often enclosed by a circlet of gold.

At first the Restoration merely continued the fashions of the Empire. The *parures* of Marie-Louise were remounted for the Duchesses of Angoulême and Berry. The Bapst ruby tiara [figure 108] is indubitably the oldest surviving mounting of the French crown jewels.

Charles X ordered for his coronation a crown which had the *Regent* at its summit, and a diamond sword [figure 101] which has happily survived the sale of the crown jewels.

Amethysts and topazes, having hitherto played only a subsidiary role, enjoyed a sudden vogue from 1800 when the *Morning Post* declared them to be preferable to all other stones for necklaces and earrings, and this entire fashion

109 One of a pair of bracelets probably made by Bapst; from the same *parure* of rubies and diamonds as the tiara [figure 108]

99

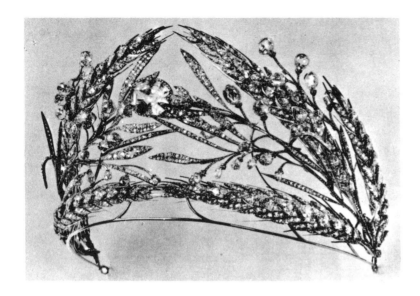

110 *(opposite)* Large amethyst *parure* set in gold, said to have belonged to a member of the Bonaparte family. French, *c.* 1820

111 and 112 *(left and below)* Tiara and aigrette of diamonds and white sapphires made by Duval for Empress Maria Feodorovna. St Petersburg, *c.* 1800

seems to have stemmed from England. The fashion took root in France about 1820 as may be seen from a large amethyst *parure* of Parisian manufacture [figure 110]; the stones are quite simply set in gold without any accompanying brilliants. The mounting itself is worked according to the 'new' method which indicates the progress already made at the beginning of the industrial age. The reliefs are obtained by mechanical stamping and finished by hand. The result was more opulent than delicate. In like manner a large quantity of small jewels suitable for the prudish and circumspect tastes of the Restoration and July monarchy were manufactured.

More than ever Parisian jewellery led the world in fashion; jewellery such as the aigrette and tiara of brilliants and white sapphires [figures 111 and 112] made at the end of the eighteenth century and in the first years of the nineteenth for the Empress Maria Feodorovna, the wife of Paul I. These pieces reflect French taste, and the tiara itself is definitely the work of Duval, a Genevan jeweller who had settled in St Petersburg. Similarly there are clear affinities

113 Diamond tiara made for Queen Theresa of
Bavaria by Kaspar Rieländer. Munich, 1832

between the ruby *parure*, mounted in 1830 by Kaspar
Rieländer, the court jeweller, for the Queen of Bavaria
[figure 130] and the tiara of the Duchess of Angoulême
[figure 108], although the Bavarian jewels show more
heaviness both in design and execution. The tiara of brilliants [figure 113] made by Rieländer in 1832 was also
part of the Bavarian treasures, and shows perfect workmanship and elegance; it was sold at Christie's in 1931.

In addition to the jewels that were ordered from native
craftsmen, foreign sovereigns frequently ordered work
directly from Parisian goldsmiths. Biennais furnished in
this way part of the regalia of the King of Bavaria (in addition to several pieces of jewellery in the ordinary meaning
of the word) and this included silver-gilt plate. He and Odiot
supplied the courts of St Petersburg, Munich, and Vienna.

England was isolated from the continent during the

greater part of the Napoleonic era but, if a little slowly, eventually followed the Parisian fashion.

The entertainments given by the Prince Regent were propitious occasions for beautiful jewellery, and the luxury of the epoch may be judged by the sapphires and brilliants in the *parure* illustrated [figure 114] which was executed between 1805 and 1810. The Prince Regent himself liked to see his lovely lady friends sumptuously dressed and contributed to this taste. Greville dining at Devonshire House in 1821 was astonished to recognize in the tiara of Lady Conyngham the Stuart sapphire, only recently returned to the royal treasury. The king continued, however, the tradition of his Hanoverian predecessors, hiring stones for his coronation regalia; the royal crown [figure 115] specially ordered for the occasion, showing the roses of England, the thistles of Scotland and the shamrock of Ireland entwined

114 *Parure* of sapphires and diamonds. English, *c.* 1805-10

103

115 Regal circlet made for the coronation of George IV (with hired stones) and remounted for Queen Victoria's coronation in 1838. Between the crosses are bunches of diamonds forming a design of the entwined rose of England, thistle of Scotland and shamrock of Ireland

116 (opposite) Diamond aigrette of Lady Cory in the form of a sprig of roses. English, nineteenth century

between its crosses was never mounted permanently in diamonds until the coronation of Victoria.

Eclecticism, the hall-mark of the nineteenth century, was soon to make itself felt in the field of jewellery, which at this period tended to seek its inspiration in the varying sources of the past. Generally speaking the first years of the century remained faithful to the antique style, but novelties were soon to appear; towards 1820 a strong tendency for imitating Nature, which did no more than prolong a trend of the eighteenth century long into the succeeding one — bouquets of flowers in jewellery which sought always to imitate the real thing more realistically. To make the illusion more complete some sprigs were mounted on 'tremblers' so that they would shake at the slightest movement of the person wearing them. In this sphere the masterpiece was the spray of lilac shown in the international exhibition of 1867 and bought by the Empress Eugénie. The craftsman whose work it was had kept a spray of real lilac before him all the time he worked on it. Around 1840 the *pampille* fashion emerged, with the flowers surrounded by showers of tiny diamonds. From 1863 onwards countless reproductions of wild roses were made, much to the distress of Massin who had

117 and 118 Pendant in the Renaissance style with figures of Aphrodite, Eros and Aeneas and Holbeinesque pendant. Gold, diamonds, enamel and pearls. Probably English, late nineteenth century

initiated the style but regretted it when he saw it cheapened. Massin's employer Fester replied to his complaints by saying: 'Well, what do you want to do? Provided that I make pointed leaves with round flowers or round leaves with pointed flowers, plenty of settings, and all at thirty *sous* that's all that is asked from me.'

More informative than the ostentatious jewellery of the time, jewels of gold, sometimes enhanced with enamel or semi-precious stones, give us a better idea of the changing fashions. The eighteenth century had closed by timidly rediscovering its forerunners in the Middle Ages. Horace Walpole, and after him, William Beckford, had castles built in the style of the Gothic Revival which the romantic era adopted and recreated in its own image complete with graceful ladies and troubadours dying of courtly love; all of this forced its way into the sphere of fashions, together with jewels *à la cathédrale*. Froment Meurice made a speciality of these and published various designs for them. His work evoked enthusiasm, and particularly from Victor Hugo who dedicated to him the following poem:

Nous sommes frères : la fleur
Par deux arts peut être faite,
Le poète est ciseleur ;
Le ciseleur est poète.

Sur son bras et sur son cou
Tu fais de tes rêveries
Statuaire du bijou,
Des palais de pierreries.

Between 1844 and 1850 A. W. Pugin provided designs of this type for a firm in Birmingham. These pieces were only remotely inspired by the medieval designs, but showed much more clearly the influence of motifs from Gothic architecture freely expressed in vignette style.

The Duchess of Berry popularized the Renaissance with her 'Quadrille de Maria-Stuart' (1829), for which the costumes were designed by Devéria, and Bapst specially remounted *parures* worth over three millions francs for the occasion, making use of the crown jewels. In the same spirit was Queen Victoria's Tudor Ball. The *Ferronière* came into fashion about 1825; it was a circlet of gold holding a jewel and worn just above the eyebrows.

Frédéric Philippi and Froment Meurice in Paris, the house of Schlichtgeroll in Vienna and others in London and Paris imitated, notably between 1835 and 1850, the pendants of the sixteenth century with some success, and their fantastic animals, centaurs and lizards [figure 135], combined with enamels and their baroque pearls were famous. Alphonse Fouquet was to keep the style alive until 1860 and beyond.

The conquest of Algeria gave birth to *mauresque* jewels, often ornamented with Arabic characters, a fashion which began in France and which was soon imitated in other countries, enjoying a vogue especially between 1840 and 1860. The canvases of Delacroix and those of the lesser known Fromentin and Ziem responded with genius to the taste for the oriental, which culminated in the faintly Turkish smoking-rooms which large hotels and even private houses began to regard as indispensable.

Towards 1826 the Italian Fortunato Pio Castellani created the first jewels executed in Rome in the antique style. He retired in 1851, but the firm bearing his name continued to produce similar work until much later. In 1860 Napoleon III bought the Campana collection which was rich in Greek, Etruscan and Roman jewels, and this proved to be an almost inexhaustible source of inspiration for jewellers; in France Fontenay drew most cleverly upon it. Photographs of Rachel as Phèdre show her wearing a diadem of metal which is ornamented with one single, large stone, like that shown in Winterhalter's portrait of the Empress Eugénie (1864).

In what we can only describe as a passion for archaeology, the second half of the nineteenth century copied Egyptian jewels [figure 126] discovered by the excavations of Mariette, and equally inspired by the news of the opening of the Suez canal. The leaders of fashion appear to have suffered no qualms about wearing these with excessively crinolined gowns designed by Worth, which openly owed their inspiration to the *paniers* of the eighteenth century.

The period had its sentimental side that produced creations which, while original, were not for all that entirely fortunate – as (by way of example) the theme of the 'bird defending its nest against the attacks of a snake' – very touching and abundantly used for nearly twenty years.

More than before brooches and medallions were employed as receptacles for portraits or for a lock of hair of some dear one, either living or departed. This passion for family relics attained its zenith in England where Queen Victoria had her children's first milk-teeth mounted in a bracelet.

She had in addition some *parures*, which while, perhaps, less dear to her maternal heart, were nonetheless more lustrous [figure 101]. Her reign began under the happiest of auspices; for her coronation in 1838 she ordered the Crown of State in which the finest stones of the royal collection were brought together – the Stuart sapphire, the sapphire of Edward the Confessor, and the ruby of the Black Prince.

The Stuart sapphire had been carried off into exile by James II and belonged to his descendants until the last of them, the Cardinal of York, put it up for sale shortly before his death in 1807 when it was bought back for the Prince Regent. St Edward's sapphire belonged according to tradition to Edward the Confessor, and the Black Prince's ruby had been part of the wealth belonging to the kings of Granada from whom it had been taken by Peter the Cruel and presented to the Black Prince in 1367 after the victory of Naveja; tradition has it that this ruby was worn by Henry V

120 (*opposite*) Imperial Crown of State, made for the coronation of Elizabeth II, reproducing that made for Queen Victoria's coronation in 1838 by Garrard. The Black Prince's ruby is on the cross above the headband, and the second *Star of Africa* has replaced the Stuart sapphire, which is now at the back of the crown

121 *(right)* Necklace with the *Timur* ruby
(352½ carats). The stone, engraved with the
names of its successive owners, was mounted
for Queen Victoria in 1849 by Garrard

122 *(opposite)* 'Reliquary' brooch made in
1855 for Empress Eugénie by Alfred Bapst.
Diamonds. The two stones in the form of a
heart in the centre of the clasp are from the
Mazarin

at the battle of Agincourt and by Richard III at Bosworth. The Crown of State was completely remounted for Elizabeth II [figure 120] reproducing almost exactly that worn by Queen Victoria, except that the second *Star of Africa*, taken from the *Cullinan* diamond, has replaced the Stuart sapphire on the centre of the frontlet.

The colonial expansion of England was to enrich the royal collection during the nineteenth century. India poured forth its wonders at the feet of its Empress. It is noteworthy, however, that these gifts were not so much the offerings of the maharajahs as gifts from the East India Company which plundered their treasures. The sack of Lahore enabled the company to offer the Queen, in 1849, the *Koh-i-Nor* and the *Timur* ruby.

The *Koh-i-Nor*, which had belonged to the Grand Mogul, was very clumsily recut, and its original weight of 800 carats was reduced to 279 carats. The *Timur* ruby [figure 121] which bore in Persian (written in Arabic characters) the names of its successive owners, Tamerlane, the Shah of Persia, the emperor Jehangir, Nader Shah, and the Maharajah Rangit Singh was mounted in a necklace.

Following the death of the Prince Consort, in 1861, the Queen retired into an austere widowhood and hardly enjoyed her treasures at all. Other crowned heads, notably the Empress Eugénie, took up again the role of leader of fashion. If some vexed spirits did not hesitate to criticize the mixed society of the Tuileries where were gathered together so many alien elements in search of amusement — rather like bankers in search of business — the sheer beauty of the Empress was beyond question as were her dresses designed by Worth and her magnificent *parures*.

In 1853 on the occasion of her marriage she had received very beautiful jewels from Napoleon III: and he himself shocked the legitimitists by wearing the diamond sword of Charles X. Almost all the *parures* remounted under the Restoration were reset by Bapst for the Empress Eugénie.

Among them were several diadems, and these included a 'Greek' model which was made to hold the *Regent* at its centre (or on certain occasions a copy of it), and was being worn by the Empress when Orsini and Pieri tried to assassinate Napoleon III at the Opera in the rue Louvois; also a 'Russian' diadem which it would appear is still preserved today in a private collection; the *parures* also included *rivières*, a corsage worked in currant leaves wrought in jewels, a comb with a shower of stones *(en pampille)*, shoulderknots or bows, various brooches — all of which were worked in diamonds. A further set consisted of several rows of enormous pearls, a diadem of pearls, brooches and bracelets of pearls and brilliants that may be seen in one of the Winterhalter portraits.

Parures of coloured stones, of which one in rubies dates from the Restoration, completed this extraordinary collection which was sold almost in its entirety by the Third Republic in 1887, evidently for political reasons. The majority of the jewels were broken up with the exception of the 'Russian' diadem and the 'reliquary' brooch [figure 122] which had been made in 1855 and had simply nothing to justify its title: the two diamonds in the form of a heart which occupy the centre of the piece are the seventeenth and eighteenth *Mazarin* diamonds, and in the seventeenth century had decorated the *justaucorps* of Louis XIV.

The International Exhibitions no less than the luxury of the imperial court did much to vaunt the supremacy of Parisian jewellery. Cheek by jowl with the older established firms such as Mellerio and Bapst (which joined with Lucien Falize in 1879) newcomers such as Cartier and Boucheron arrived with the prospect of a fine future.

From the end of the eighteenth century the jewellers had been installed at the Palais-Royal, but in the mid nineteenth century they removed to Place Vendôme and rue de la Paix.

Russian princesses, nabobs, and boyars came to admire

123 *(opposite)* Diamond necklace. French, *c.* 1760

the latest novelties of fashion. Some maharajahs brought stones from India in strong boxes, and had them mounted in Paris for themselves, for their wives and even for their elephants.

The first stones from the newly discovered South African mines were placed on the market in Paris in 1869, furnishing jewellers with bigger and more abundant stones. From then onwards mountings became lighter, so that the ideal became to make the mounting as invisible as possible – the *monture illusion* took root and was general by the last quarter of the century, by which time the mountings were completely invisible.

In order to achieve this result new metals were employed for the setting of the stones. Since the seventeenth century silver had become a traditional setting but from the mid nineteenth century onwards gold became the preferred setting – not without some resistance being put up. Vever, writing as recently as 1906, said: 'Great pieces of jewellery will never cease to be set in silver'. Now we see he was wrong, for platinum, even more solid, has tended to oust gold.

The largest diamond known to date, the *Cullinan*, was presented by the Government of the Transvaal to Edward VII, and from it came both the first and the second *Stars of Africa* to ornament the Crown of State and the royal sceptre of England.

This was the epoch when Queen Alexandra created the royal style in England. Before her queens and princesses had adopted for daytime wear town *toilette* similar to those of their fashionable contemporaries, reserving their magnificence for court balls. Alexandra, doubtless tired of the perpetual mourning of her mother-in-law, created for official ceremonies a fabulous style, emphasising in the public eye all the majesty of royalty, appearing in light colours and splendid dress, her hair dressed with aigrettes of feathers, her throat wrapped round with enormous pearls, and sparkling with diamonds [figure 124].

124 Photograph of Queen Alexandra as Princess of Wales (*c.* 1889). She is wearing an aigrette of feathers, a pendant and a 'dog-collar' of pearls and diamonds

114

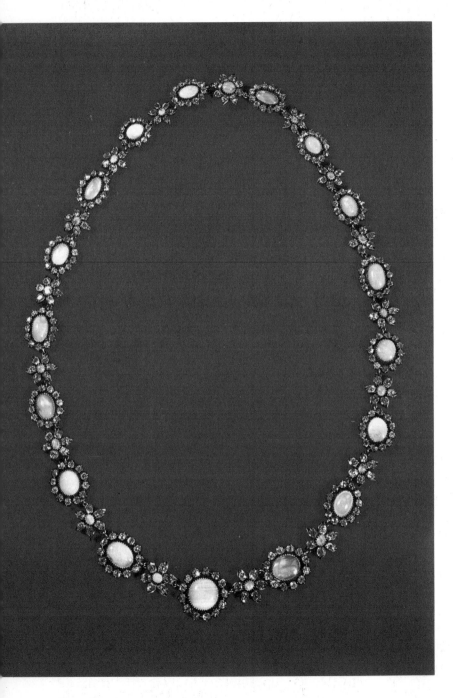

125 *(left)* Necklace of opals and brilliants, formerly belonging to the Maréchale de Rochambeau. End of the eighteenth century

126 *(opposite) Parure* in the Egyptian style. Gold, agate, onyx and jade. Italian, *c.* 1860

127 and 128 Tiara and necklace made for Queen Maria-Pia of Portugal by Estevas de Souza. Gold and diamonds. Lisbon, 1878

This fashion was immediately taken up by the majority of the crowned heads of the period, and faithfully kept to by such few of them who have survived. At this time only the court of Russia could rival that of England either in number or luxury of its *parures*. The tiara and necklace [figures 127 and 128] made by Estevas de Souza for Queen Maria-Pia of Portugal is, nevertheless, perfect in its elegance.

Such important pieces were often mounted in a severely classical style which has never really gone out of fashion, such as the tiara of the dukes of Westminster [figure 131] which comprises diamonds that belonged to Queen Charlotte, of which the largest central stone had been hired out for the coronation of George IV.

Women of the world were not the only ones to make a display of magnificent jewels, for in the second half of the nineteenth century and the beginning of the twentieth courtesans occupied a position of great importance in the demi-monde, and the *parures* which they wore for their photographs testifies to this. William III of the Netherlands gave Elisa Parker the *de la Croix* diamond (41 carats) from the crown of Naples. After 1870 Mme de Paiva bought a

129 *(opposite)* Portrait of the Empress
Josephine by Gérard. She is wearing a *parure*
of diamonds, emeralds and pear-shaped pearls

130 *(above)* Tiara of rubies and brilliants
made for Queen Theresa of Bavaria by
Rieländer. Munich, 1830

131 Diamond tiara of the Dukes of Westminster. The central stone was
used in George IV's crown at his coronation and the two pearshaped
diamonds were presented to Queen Charlotte by the Nabob of Arcot.
English, second half of the nineteenth century

tiara of the Empress who had once refused her admission to the Tuileries. The white pearls of Léonide Leblanc and the black pearls of Cora Pearl were famous. At the close of the century the jewel caskets of Liane de Pougy [figure 133] and Caroline Otero [figure 132] provoked astonishment from even the most hardened free-livers. They had been made up of successive gifts by various admirers, with no thought of continuing the same trends as their predecessors, so that the sole fault of such collections was their lack of homogeneity. Among the demi-monde those gems became the object of fierce jealousies, and one may recall the gesture of Liane de Pougy, who learnt that Otero intended to dine at Maxim's wearing every single jewel she possessed (out of incontrollable vanity) for in the course of a rapid career Otero had accumulated a great number, including a necklace that had belonged to the Empress Eugénie; Liane de Pougy allowed the beautiful Spaniard to make a sensation, then Liane entered herself dressed in a simple white dress without a single ornament, without even a ring; she was closely followed by her maid bending under a burden of diamonds.

The easygoing climate of the *Belle Epoque* was followed by the decadence of *fin-de-siècle* art. Tormented souls enjoyed an exquisite morbidity; fantastic ecstasies and anxieties were dreamed up. Jewels, particularly precious stones, exercised an irresistible attraction. After Des Esseintes, Dorian Grey rediscovered in ancient texts the symbolic meaning of jewels and the splendid, costly *parures* of the cruel princes of the Renaissance. In his exasperated refinement Huysmans' hero is contemptuous of the diamond as 'singularly vulgar for even tradesmen wear it on their little finger'; emeralds and rubies remind him only of the 'green and red eyes of some bus whose signal lights blaze out in these two colours'; the amethyst is condemned as being 'dishonoured by the ruddy ears and the chubby hands of butchers' wives'. In place of all these 'too civilized and too well-known' stones he prefers 'more surprising and more bizarre

132 Caroline Otero

133 Liane de Pougy

123

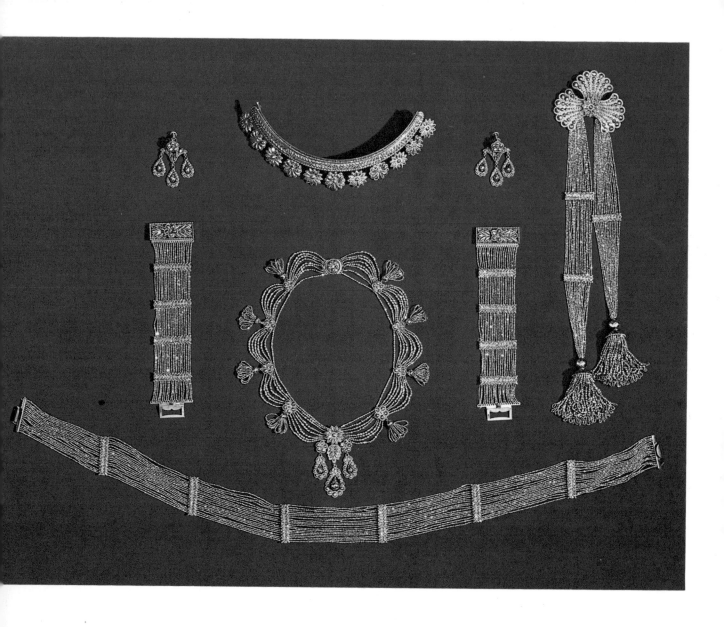

134 *Parure* of cut steel, with tiara, necklace,
bracelets, ear-rings, and girdle with a tassel.
Late eighteenth century

135 Brooch in the form of a lizard. Diamonds
and emeralds. English, *c.* 1835

136 (below) Pendant, 'Sylvia' by Henri Vever.
Gold, enamel, brilliants, rubies and agate.
Paris, 1900

137 (right) Necklace by René Lalique. Gold,
enamel, diamonds and chrysolite, Paris, 1900

138 (opposite) Pendant in the form of a
nymph by L. Gautrait. Gold, enamel, diamond
and pearls French, c. 1900

minerals' — whose names at least, possess some charm for
him — cat's-eyes from Ceylon, cymophane, sapphirine, boast-
ing of their 'mysterious and perverse sparkling', chrysoberyl,
hyacinthe and so on. It was the surfeit that made the whole
thing sicken and die.

Some great ladies, but mostly the women of the theatre
and courtesans, attracted by the bizarre and anxious to please
the young intellectuals, adopted a seductive and twisted
form of jewellery that Vever, Fouquet, Lalique in Paris, and
Tiffany in New York were offering them. Here were to be
found the themes of the *art nouveau*. Botanic motifs were
common, lianas writhed in demented convulsions, iris, pop-
pies, mistletoe; faces of women of 'fatal beauty', now dedicated, now radiating troubled sensuality, emerge from dis-
ordered tresses; the variegated wing of a dragonfly and
Byzantine peacocks' eyes dazzle with iridescence. But above
all it was the snake theme that fascinated the *fin de siècle*,
which was attracted by its evil portents. It formed the chief
motif of the Fouquet bracelet [figure 139] made after a
drawing by Mucha for Sarah Bernhardt, who wore it in her
role of Cleopatra, and who had so much difficulty in paying
the jeweller that he was obliged to send a messenger to the

theatre every night where she was appearing in order to collect the instalments she owed on it.

The majority of the jewellers of the *art nouveau* only used traditional precious stones as accessories, like Des Esseintes preferring rare coloured stones, baroque pearls and especially enamelled settings with their finely executed workmanship, in the good pieces at least. Unfortunately the work of the masters was frequently imitated clumsily, vulgarly and heavily in many industrial reproductions.

The 1914—18 war, and even more that of 1939—45, together with the advance of socialism have brought a number of severe shocks to the jeweller's art. Even in countries where royalty has survived, the court life which had given birth to the splendours of this art has practically disappeared, and it is only for exceptional occasions that jewellers are required to set *grandes parures* for evening wear. Those which some great families still possess repose for the most part in their strong-boxes and date mostly from the second half of the nineteenth century; some, more sadly still, take the road to the auction rooms, and finish by being broken up. The grand dukes have died in wretchedness, the maharajahs, recluses in their palaces, are hardly concerned with mounting the stones they have preserved; the South Americans generally consecrate less time and less money to *la vie parisienne* than did the heroes of Offenbach's day.

In the Middle East the oil-kings hide their wealth in their harems, and only the Americans remain; beautiful American women still dream of diamonds 'as big as the Ritz', and of 'breakfast at Tiffany's'.

In spite of the obliterating taxes some of them are able to make their dreams come true, and some of the most beautiful jewels of Europe have crossed the Atlantic to be worn by millionaires' wives in Texas or New York. But if a diamond remains for a woman 'a joy for ever' the majority of them have to content themselves with their engagement ring — generally quite ordinary.

For those of average means cultured pearls have practically replaced those from the Orient, and frequently costume-jewels are the only ones which a woman who is concerned with her appearance can afford. If they do not have the perfection of the creations of the great jewellers of the rue de la Paix or Fifth Avenue such jewels at least provide complete liberty in their choice of materials, human imagination being more fertile than the resources of classical mineralogy, and these bear witness to remarkable and constantly new invention. Their intrinsic value and their durability is very ephemeral, like that of the *toilette* for which they have been conceived. Even so for that reason they still indicate the history of the fashion. Their French name reveals at once their graces and their weak point: *bijoux de fantaisie*. They are too charming not to attract and too fragile, doubtless, ever to hold a lasting place in history.

139 Bracelet made by Georges Fouquet after a drawing by Mucha for Sarah Bernhardt, and worn by her in the role of Cleopatra. Gold, enamel, opals, rubies, emeralds and diamonds. 1906

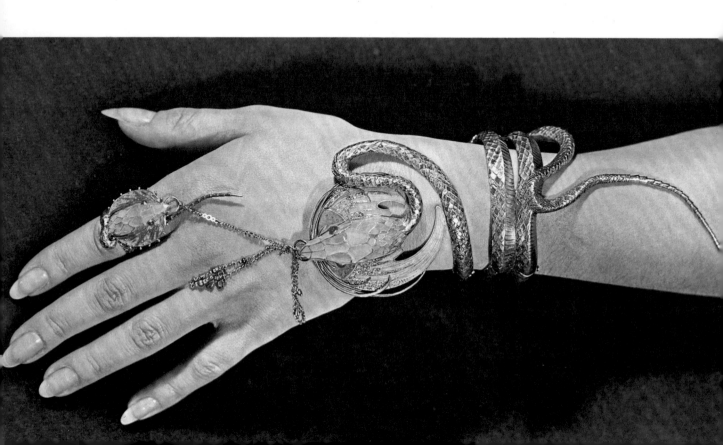